Live for a Change

Live for a Change

DISCOVERING AND USING YOUR GIFTS

Francis Dewar

DARTON·LONGMAN+TODD

First published in 1988 by
Darton, Longman and Todd Ltd
1 Spencer Court
140–142 Wandsworth High Street
London SW18 4JJ

Reprinted four times

This edition published 1999

© 1988 and 1999 Francis Dewar

The right of Francis Dewar to be identified as the Author of this work
has been asserted in accordance with the Copyright, Designs and
Patents Act 1988.

ISBN 0–232–52349–5

A catalogue record for this book is available from
the British Library

Phototypeset by Intype London Ltd
Printed and bound in Great Britain by
Page Bros, Norwich, Norfolk.

To the many people who have helped and supported me on my journey, and especially Elizabeth, my wife, friend and companion on the way, one of whose gifts is for enabling others.

Contents

Preface to the Second Edition ix
Preface to the First Edition xi
Acknowledgements xiv

1. Introduction 1
2. Look Out 11
3. Enquire Within 20
4. Be Still and Know 30
5. Know God 41
6. What Might it Mean to Follow Christ? 48
7. Listen to Your Story 61
8. 'Disabilities' Might Become Gifts 72
9. Know Yourself to be Loved by God 79
10. Know Your Gifts and Leanings 92
11. Know the World's Needs, Feel the World's Pain 103
12. Dream Dreams 115
13. Hear a Call 126
14. Feeling Inadequate 148
15. Get into Action 154
16. How Could the Church Help? 172
17. Counting the Cost 184

Postscript 189
Appendix 190
Other Books by Francis Dewar 207

Preface to the second edition

People sometimes tell me that this book has changed their lives. When it has, it is because they have done the exercises which form its kernel. The book is based on a weekly evening course which I have offered from time to time during the last twenty years. In the mid-1980s people who lived too far away to come to it used to ask if there was a version available for use at home. This was my response. So it is primarily designed for individual use.

But in the eleven years since it was first published many readers have used it with others in a group. If that is possible for you, I do very much recommend it. There is a great deal to be gained from mutual listening, support and encouragement. I have enlarged the appendix with a view to assisting you to do that. The body of the book has, where necessary, been brought up to date; and I have added some extra material, including two new chapters.

I am grateful to Charles Foister, Mary Lewis, Mary Wilson and David Wood (the Trustees of the Journey Inward, Journey Outward Project), and to my wife, Elizabeth, who offered suggestions; and in particular to Charles and Elizabeth who read all or part of the new material.

FRANCIS DEWAR

Preface to the first edition

If you have done the same job for many years, you may become aware of a quiet little voice inside you which whispers: 'Do I really want to go on doing this day after day, year after year, until I retire?' You may ignore it or suppress it. But it is the voice of your hidden self. Buried within you lie all kinds of possibilities and capabilities that do not find expression in your present way of life and work. Only by listening to it will you get any hint of what those possibilities might be.

If you have spent the last twenty-five years bringing up children and have loyally put the needs of your family first, you will probably have suppressed your own feelings and needs so often that you have lost touch with them. You do not know what you want for yourself any more. When the children leave home, suddenly you are faced with the question: 'What is my life for now?' An increasing number of people are faced very abruptly with this question by being made redundant and finding they are unable to get another job.

The requirements of job and family make demands which govern most of our active life, especially in younger adulthood. It is easy to find yourself living very largely by reaction to what happens. We tend to live much more from the outside inwards, as it were, rather than from within outwards. We do not often look within us for the springs of our action. We do not act out of an inner stillness. Rather, we *re*act to what others do or to what others demand.

There is nothing wrong with this up to a point. It is not only unavoidable but desirable – some of the time. It is when it happens all the time that it becomes destructive.

It destroys that root of inner initiative and creativity that arises deep within us, which can be so fruitful for others when it flowers as well as offering great personal satisfaction and fulfilment.

Within each individual lie particular possibilities, gifts and qualities that are not called into play, either because of low self-esteem or unfavourable circumstances, or because they are not saleable enough or the person is not in touch enough with her own deep centre to be aware of their existence. I think of these as a kind of treasure buried away out of sight of society, out of sight even of the 'owner'. God calls each of us to bring out and enact our treasure for the enrichment of others in some specific way at each stage of our life. The activity and initiative that this will require of you will vary widely from person to person. For one it may be an aspect of a job they are paid for. For another it may be some spare-time task. For one it may be an enterprise measured in hours; for another, one measured in weeks or years. But whatever its context or its scope, it will be something new, breaking new ground, an initiative that you take unbidden, an activity that you conceive and put in hand unasked.

The world is in many ways a wilderness, and so are the hearts of many people. In the deserts of our inmost selves tiny seeds could germinate for the enrichment of the deserts around us. In our country, for example, people in inner cities and housing estates are beset by poverty – of cash, of housing, of amenities, of relationships, of work, of meaning. Even in leafier districts people are impoverished in heart and in spirit, if not in more material ways. Many people, as Thoreau put it, lead lives of quiet desperation. The ancient Hebrew prophet Isaiah dreamed of the desert blossoming like the rose. The rose is a symbol of wholeness, of integration and fulfilment for individuals, of shalom – that is, of peace and human flourishing – for the world. It is my belief that in every one of us these possibilities lie dormant, waiting to grow and flower to enrich the lives of others.

So this is a 'do-it-yourself' book to encourage you to

search for your treasure, or, if you prefer it, to help your tiny seed to germinate. There is within you what someone has called 'a younger, truer self'. This is not your inner child of the past, the child you once were. Rather it is something which could grow in the future. Each of us, responsive to God, has a younger truer self to conceive and nurture, a person to be, a task to do, a gift to give.

There is an old proverb, 'Hear and forget; see and remember; do and understand.' The backbone of this book is formed by the exercises at the end of each chapter. These were devised or chosen first, and are based on some years' experience of running courses on this theme. The book was constructed around them. If you read it without doing the exercises, I hope you will find it interesting: but it will be like being taken out to a restaurant and forgoing the main course. Doing them yourself is the meat of the book. The rest is appetiser.

One other thing perhaps needs to be said at the outset. I write from a Christian standpoint, in the hope that we can somehow make fruitful for today the spiritual riches of our nation and culture. But I venture to hope that what I offer may be of use to any seeker after truth.

I want to thank the many people who in one way or another have helped me with this book: Joan Trowbridge who did the typing; Maude Henderson, Margaret Kane and Billy Jackson who read the first draft and made many helpful suggestions; and in particular Chris Austwick, Wendy Byatt, Angela Cunningham, Elaine Dunning, Mary Dyke, Pat Francis, Suzie Morel, Donald and Moira Tate, Gillian Widdows and Jenny Wormald who acted as 'guinea-pigs' and worked with the material of the book as it was being written. After a few chapters one of them commented that working through each section was like unwrapping a present. I hope that you may find it so too.

FRANCIS DEWAR

Acknowledgements

The illustration in Chapter 3 was drawn by Gill Muller, those in Chapters 7, 14 and 15 by Paul Judson, and those in Chapters 9, 12 and 13 by Elizabeth Dewar. I drew the one for Chapter 1.

I am grateful to the following for permission to quote copyright material: Bruno Cassirer, from *Zorba the Greek* by Nikos Kazantsakis; Darton, Longman & Todd, from *God of Surprises* by Gerard W. Hughes; Sister Ann Maureen Gallagher IHM for her poem 'The Time for Figs'; Editions Gallimard, from *Mythes, Rêves et Mystères* by Mircea Eliade © Editions Gallimard 1957; Harper & Row, from *Doorways to Christian Growth* by J. McMakin and R. Nary © 1984 Jacqueline McMakin and Rhoda Nary; William Heinemann, from *The Velveteen Rabbit* by Margery Williams; Peter Lomas, from his *True and False Experience*; Mowbrays, from *Dance in the Dark* by Sydney Carter (originally published by Mowbrays as *The Rock of Doubt* in 1978); Paulist Press, from *Keeping your Personal Journal* by G. F. Simons © 1978 George F. Simons; World Peacemakers, from *Handbook for World Peacemaker Groups* by Gordon Cosby and Bill Price; Brian Wren, for his parable of the factory.

A note about inclusive language
God is personal but beyond gender, and the ascription of gender or even parenthood to God is a metaphor, though it can be a helpful one. This means that personal pronouns *can* be a problem, and a sensitive issue for some. I have tried where possible to avoid ascribing either gender to God. But it is not always possible, and in the case of quotations I have left personal pronouns unaltered.

1

Introduction

A friend who had recently been made redundant complained: 'I like routine, to have clear guidelines, to know what I am supposed to do with my time.' It is not only a job that provides a structure for your time. In the first thirty years or so of your life there are many voices to tell you what to do, what to believe, how to live, what goals to go for, what prizes to strive for. The first half of life involves testing the authenticity of some of these voices. It means living some of what they suggest, and in doing so discovering what is worthwhile and what is in the end unimportant. But in the process you take on all kinds of responsibilities, to people, to a job, to a building society, to finance companies, to your own self-image, which restrict your freedom to change. Who you are becomes defined by your obligations, and by others' expectations, by what you could call outer considerations.

But there is more to you than this. You have all kinds of feelings that for one reason or another you do not express. There are things that it is best not to say at your place of work if you want to keep your job. There are feelings that you suppress at home if you want to keep your friends. These are, as it were, the surface features of another side of your character, a part of you that you do not show to others. You may think of it as a part of you that you do not want to reveal to others, and you may be right as far as ordinary practical living is concerned. But this other side of you has also a very positive aspect. I would go so far as to say that it contains some of your most creative and valuable possibilities.

We are not just what other people see of us. We are not even just what we know of ourselves. There lie hidden within us enormous creative possibilities of which we are largely unaware. Most of us do only a fraction of what we are capable of doing. Part of the reason is that we live too much by what is expected of us. We allow our lives to be governed too much by outer factors. The inner aspects of our nature receive scant attention or are neglected altogether. In fact in this country if you mention to your friends that you are doing some inner exploration they may give you a funny look and warn you against being morbid and introspective. Those two words are frequently bracketed together by those who live by standard reach-me-down opinions: looking within is something to be avoided as slightly indecent, and certainly not to be encouraged.

I hope I can persuade you otherwise, at least enough to give yourself a chance to listen to some of your inner wisdom and take it a little more seriously. At this stage I am not suggesting that you act upon it – but that you listen to what it has to say.

The chapter themes outline some aspects of the process of looking for your treasure. There may be others; but these are the ones I have found personally to be important.

'Listen to your feelings'. Chapters 1 to 3 provide a way into this, beginning with your daily activities. I shall be drawing attention to the extent to which what we do and feel is defined by others, and shall be encouraging you to notice what *you* feel about what you do; Chapter 7 takes this a bit deeper. *As you do the exercises, write down your feelings and musings in a private jottings book.* Expressing your feelings and reflecting on your experience in this way will help to give your inner promptings more substance, without rushing prematurely into speech or action. So write down your hopes and fears, your angers and frustrations, your fantasies and whims, your dreams of the night as well as the day, the things you would like to say to others that are not possible or not diplomatic, the things you want to say to God, the things you seem to hear God say to you. This kind of private notebook or journal is a very helpful aid on your journey, especially at times of change in your life. Reading it over later can give you a sense of perspective and help you to be aware of what is important to you and what is more transient.

'Be still and know' (Chapter 4) encourages you to make space in your life for quietness and inactivity, and suggests this as an essential ingredient in being open to God. It is my belief that the creative initiatives in life come from God. It is therefore important to cultivate an attitude of receptivity and restrain the desire to be active and in control all the time. It may be that you have difficulty with 'God' language. If you believe that the source of our creativity, compassion and longing is somehow beyond our comprehension, and yet draws us on to strive to give it expression, then perhaps you can make the necessary adjustment when I use 'God' language. You could formulate the aim of this book as encouraging you to work with the question, 'What is your life for?' I would express that question as 'What is God calling you to do with your energies?' because to the source of our energy, to the animator of our creative initiatives and to the goal of our deepest longings, I ascribe the name God.

'Know God' as s/he is, is the theme of Chapters 5 and 6. I grew up with the notion that God was a kind of celestial taskmaster. Christianity was about doing your duty. It went without saying that such duties would be unwelcome and unpleasant, imposed from the outside on an unwilling heart. In fact it was assumed that if you enjoyed them they were probably not really Christian. It is important to see past false images like this if we are to discover God as profoundly loving, and as the source of all creativity and joy in living. In a similarly off-putting way, Jesus is sometimes presented as impossibly good, or possessed of magical powers beyond anything ordinary mortals could aspire to. If we can dispense with this spurious idol we may find him an ever-present inner guide and companion.

'Listen to your story'. Chapter 7 is about becoming more aware of your life as a series of events with an underlying meaning which connects with the essence of who you are and points towards the tasks that are uniquely yours to do. But we are prisoners of our past: there may be a lot of work to do to free ourselves enough to be able to move into the future in trust and hope.

Chapter 8, ' "Disabilities" might become gifts', draws attention to the fact that most of us are aware of problems, or handicaps, or flaws in our character. Such things, as we work at accepting and absorbing them, often turn out to be very important factors in our search for what God might be inviting us to offer to others.

'Know yourself to be loved by God'. Chapter 9 is for those who find it difficult to realise that God loves them, or who need to let the love of God seep through to the deeper and less acceptable layers of their nature.

Chapter 10, 'Know your gifts and leanings', suggests some ways of identifying your aptitudes.

Up to this point we are mainly concerned with a journey inwards. Chapter 11, 'Know the world's needs', begins to look outwards. If what you do is to enrich the lives of others, you need knowledge of how people are ground down, what they have to put up with, and what the causes of this are. You will be deaf to God's calling if you are blind to what happens to people. If God calls you at the point of your gifts it will probably be at the point of someone else's pain or impoverishment. God is, after all, biased towards the impoverished.

'Dream dreams'. Most of us are not practised in this, or we use it as escapism. Chapter 12 encourages you to dream in a more purposeful way, and to glimpse a little of God's dream for his creation.

'Hear a call' and 'Feeling inadequate'. The topics of Chapters 13 and 14 often go hand in hand. What God longs for for us is always beyond our wildest imaginings. The part in it that he calls us to play always feels beyond our powers.

'Get into action'. Chapter 15 suggests that an essential part of exploring is in doing, in taking a step in the direction you seem to be discerning. Action helps clarify your sense of direction.

'Get confirmation from others'. Inward calls need confirmation or we open the door to zealots and cranks. One of the functions of the Church could be to offer people who think they are called to a particular task a second opinion. But the Church has a narrow, ecclesiastical, and professionalised notion of what God calls people to do. Some drastic changes of attitude are needed at all levels of the Church's life, and Chapter 16 makes some suggestions about this.

Finally, Chapter 17, 'Counting the cost', reminds you that if you desire to follow this road, there is a price to be paid: though many would say that it is small compared to the rewards. (You could with advantage look at this chapter sooner, perhaps between Chapters 10 and 11.)

I have listed these aspects in chapter order: but do not attach too much importance to that. It is not a matter of one aspect being dealt with before you go on to the next. In fact 'dealt with' is too summary a phrase for the interlocking features of what is a continuing process. Like threads being woven into a fabric, the pattern becomes discernible only gradually. See the diagram on page 6.

Do not be surprised if you find it a slow process. For example 'Knowing yourself to be loved by God' is an ever-deepening process which may take a lifetime. 'Dreaming dreams' is not something you do once and for all: it means keeping alive your capacity to see and to be captivated by what could be. 'Hearing a call' is not, for most people, an unchanging call to some lifelong activity: as you respond God calls you on to new tasks. As you know your gifts better and understand the real needs of the world better, you will be better able to hear how God is calling you to put the one at the service of the other. As you know yourself to be loved and treasured by God, so the treasure that you are is more available to be a gift for others.

So this book is not intended to be read straight through. It is designed to be used as a stimulus for your own reflection and searching. Give yourself time to try the exercises. Use it to mull over from time to time, rather than devouring it as though to acquire information.

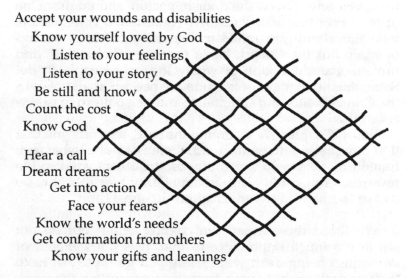

Accept your wounds and disabilities
   Know yourself loved by God
     Listen to your feelings
    Listen to your story
   Be still and know
  Count the cost
 Know God

 Hear a call
Dream dreams
  Get into action
   Face your fears
  Know the world's needs
Get confirmation from others
   Know your gifts and leanings

It could also be used by a small group of people who would undertake the exercises and meet each week to report how they got on. One of the reviewers of this book commented, 'For those who have for long faced the world with the traditional English stiff upper lip, the sheer strength of feelings uncovered during the inward journey may be very dismaying if we are left to face and to deal with them unsupported. I think it would always be wise to seek time and space to Live for a Change in a situation where we can draw on others, directly or indirectly, for support and so find the nerve actually *to* change. Wise, too, to plan that waiting for us "at home" is at least one person with whom we can share as much as we wish of what we have uncovered for ourselves.' Even if you are not using the book with a group, it will be a great help to have someone you can meet with periodically with whom you can share your experience of doing the exercises and what it has brought to your awareness.

If you decide to meet with a group, read the Appendix first. Some of the exercises could also be done in a group setting but, please note, they are not designed to be used as a basis for discussion. Each person should have an opportunity to share their own experience or reflection, but there should be no discussion of the rights or wrongs of it. Discussion, as opposed to sharing, is liable to lead to notions that there is a 'proper way' to feel or react; but that will take you away from an awareness of God's leading. The danger of all groups is that a pattern of expectation easily gets established. That is why the exercises are offered first to be done by individuals: then, if you like, you can share with others what you did and what you found. But if you do, both you and the others will need to grow in your capacity to listen. Any group life that is to do justice to the infinite variety of human possibility needs to start from a willingness to be open to, and to listen to, its individual members, and that means being receptive to the unfamiliar and the non-standard. As it happens, that willingness is also a prime prerequisite for being open to God's calling. God is nothing if not unexpected.

One of the aspects mentioned in the outline is the import-ance of dreaming dreams. One of my dreams is that in every church congregation, or at least in every district, there would be a small group of people who would offer one another support and encouragement in what I have called the inward journey, so that they could be, as it were, midwives to one another, helping to bring to birth each one's 'baby'. But it is not something that church committees can lay on or plan for. If you want to see it happen, it will need to start with you. You could invite one or two people who you think might be responsive, either from your con-gregation or from a wider circle, to meet you to explore this possibility. You do not have to be experienced in leading small groups. All you need is the willingness to learn to listen, to your own heart and to the others who will join you. It is the willingness to listen that is all-important. It is to people like you that this book is offered as a modest tool-kit for beginning a personal search.

AN EXERCISE

Make a list of the 'hats' that you wear in your daily life, the different roles and activities you engage in.

Then take some coloured felt-tip pens and draw yourself wearing each hat. You do not have to be an artist. Drawing is a way of expressing things that can help to reach beyond words, even if you only draw pin-people. Play around with the idea of a hat as the symbol of each role that you occupy. For example, one of my roles is 'preacher': in this hat, I draw myself standing in a pulpit with a halo over my head. Or, instead of yourself wearing a hat, you could draw a different kind of symbol of the role, one that encapsulates your feeling about it. One of my roles is DIY person: I draw that as a stepladder, to me a boring and uninspiring object. Much of the time I feel bored and uninspired by the DIY activities I do around the house.

When you have drawn yourself in each hat, jot down beside each drawing words or phrases which express your feelings as you occupy that role. Do not be surprised if you have both positive and negative feelings about the same hat. And do be honest with yourself. Even if you are meeting in a group to share your experience as you do these exercises, there is no obligation to tell all. The first and most important thing is to be honest with yourself; then you can decide how much you feel comfortable about sharing or describing to the others.

In this hat I feel
imprisoned
eloquent
insulated
out of place

A PARABLE FOR THE READER

There was once a man who wanted to know more about jade. One day he discovered in conversation that a friend of his knew someone who was an expert. 'Oh,' he said, 'do you think you could introduce me to him so that I can get some lessons?' So his friend arranged for him to meet the expert and a series of ten lessons was arranged at what seemed a reasonable price.

On the day of the first lesson the man arrived at the expert's house and was shown into a comfortable, light, airy room. The expert handed him a piece of jade and then left, closing the door behind him. The man looked idly at the greenish stone, and wondered how long it would be before the expert returned and the lesson could start. Half an hour went by. Then the expert returned and announced that that was the end of the day's lesson and he would see him at the same time next week.

The man went home a bit mystified. Anyway, the next week he came back and the same thing happened. The expert ushered him in, gave him a piece of jade and withdrew without any explanation. Half an hour later he came back and said that that was the end of the lesson.

This happened each week for several weeks. The man was beginning to feel cheated. He reckoned he was paying good money for nothing. A few days later he happened to meet his friend who had recommended the expert, and told him what he thought about the lessons, and that he was given no instruction at all. 'All he does is just hand me a piece of jade and then he disappears', he complained, 'and blow me,' he went on, 'last time he had the cheek to give me a fake!'

2

Look Out

A few years ago I resigned my position as vicar of a
parish in order to start what has come to be called
the Journey Inward, Journey Outward project. One of my
daughters, then still at school, used to have difficulty in
answering questions like: 'What does your dad do?' She
would come home and say to me wistfully, 'Dad, I wish
you'd go back to being a proper vicar.' The fact is that in
my work I do not occupy a ready-made role any more.
There is no clear standard label that would immediately
communicate to people what I do. In the first few months
after leaving the parish I was not too sure what I was
doing either. I felt the lack of a framework of activity. I
think I felt a bit what it is like to be unemployed, though
without the pain and rejection of being made redundant. I
remember a deanery synod meeting at the time, when
being introduced as 'supernumerary' did give me a taste
of the feeling of being nobody because I did not have a
'job'.

Unemployment and the question marks it puts against
the significance of work in our lives forms part of the
backdrop for our theme. In fact this whole book is in a
small way a contribution to the current debate about the
future of work. How important a place is work likely to
have in our lives in the future? How important a place
should it have? For our purpose here I just want to draw

attention briefly to two common assumptions about work which stand in the way of people discovering their inner treasure. Both are called in question by current levels of unemployment.

The first is that work is something you are given by others, not something you initiate. Since the industrial revolution most jobs have been defined or laid down by others because of the large-scale nature of manufacturing processes and of the economic framework that goes with them. At most places of work you do not have much say in what should be done, or how it should be done. That is decided for you. That can be true even if you run a corner shop or are a senior manager in a large company. The 'others' in this case will be the market. The market dictates what you can or cannot do. So jobs for most people are in one way or another defined and directed by others. When you take a job, in return for doing 'their thing their way' and sacrificing some, or even all, of your autonomy, you receive a wage. In effect you sell a portion of your time; and perhaps part of yourself.

You may feel that this is more true of wage-earners than others. That may be so. In my experience of parish work and meeting and talking to people of different backgrounds, I believe it is more widely true than we might like to think. The majority of people would not go to work if they were not paid. Basically they go to earn a living, to be able to support themselves and their dependants, and not because they enjoy the work so much that they would do it anyway, even if it was unpaid. In other words most people do not feel that their work is in any sense an expression of their inner nature. It is imposed on them from the outside. And the changes in the nature of work in the last two hundred years have increased this 'alienated' quality of much of our daily work.

At the beginning of the machine age William Blake wrote: 'We would endure a profound hurt in serving systems and not being able to find our own deep centres.' His prophecy has come only too true. Most people in industrialised societies are out of touch with their own deep centres, their inner selves. This is especially true when it comes to our daily activity, what we do with our time. So deep has this assumption become that it affects our activities even outside the sphere of paid work. Many of us can hardly conceive what our daily activity would be if it was not *demanded* of us, *expected* of us, or at least *asked* of us by someone else. The self-starter is missing. Most of the time we live by reaction to what comes at us, instead of living from the inside outwards, from our still centre.

The second assumption about work that grips our society is that who you are is defined by your job. If you ask someone what he is, you do not expect an answer like 'person' or 'human being' but 'fitter and turner' or 'computer programmer'. D. H. Lawrence puts this pointedly in a conversation piece:

What is he?
– A man, of course.
Yes, but what does he do?
– He lives and is a man.
Oh quite! but he must work. He must have a job of
    some sort.
– Why?
Because obviously he's not one of the leisured classes.
– I don't know. He has lots of leisure. And he makes
    quite beautiful chairs.
There you are then! He's a cabinet maker.
– No no!
Anyhow a carpenter and joiner.
– Not at all.
But you said so.
– What did I say?
That he made chairs, and was a joiner and carpenter.
– I said he made chairs, but I did not say he was a
    carpenter.
All right then, he's just an amateur.
– Perhaps! Would you say that a thrush was a pro-
    fessional flautist, or just an amateur?
I'd say it was just a bird.

– And I say he is just a man.
All right! You always did quibble.
('What is he?' from *The Selected Poems of D. H.
Lawrence*, ed. J. Reeves, Heinemann, 1967)

Nowadays so much is your identity tied up with your paid
work that when you lose your job you feel you are not a
person any more.

Both these assumptions are more widely questioned now
because of high unemployment levels for men in recent
years; their power has of course been felt by women for
much longer. It is notorious that housework does not count
as work; and women at home are only too familiar with
not being regarded as persons in their own right.

My belief and hope is that the fact that unemployment
and the insecurity of many jobs are now 'issues' could help
wean us from these two attitudes. We could move away,
as a society and as individuals, from the work ethic – the
view that hard work is good for you regardless of whether
it is any kind of expression of what you are. The whole
question of the purpose of work and the proportion of our
time and energy that it demands is wide open. I would
like to see a move towards what has been called a contribution ethic. I would like to see all our citizens enabled to
recognise and make use of their gifts regardless of whether
'the market' will pay for them. This will involve large
changes – in attitudes to work, in education and in the
way the 'unemployed' are treated and paid.

Unemployment then, or the threat of it, and the issue of
meaning in daily activity, form part of the backdrop for
the theme of this book. Another part of the background
against which all our lives are lived today is the threat of
nuclear war and global environmental damage. The rele-
vance of our theme to these issues could be stated in one
sentence. If we blow ourselves up or damage the world
eco-system beyond repair it will be because not enough
people have found enough genuine meaning and fulfilment in their daily life and activity. Human beings without
enough to live for become a danger to themselves and

others. Making money and the exercise of power
substitutes for living. The issue of meaning is th̲ ̲ ̲.₀re
crucial for the very survival of life on our planet.

Finding your way back to being in touch with your deep
centre is a slow process. Here is a dream a man had as
part of that process in his own life. He tells it in his own
words:

> A man was running in a race. There were thousands
> of spectators. Round and round the track they went,
> seemingly without end. He kept in the lead, but only
> just. Suddenly he fell to the ground. I was astounded
> and horrified. Surely this couldn't be; he *must* win. I
> ran over to him. But to my surprise he hadn't actually
> collapsed involuntarily: he had decided he wasn't
> going to continue driving himself on just for the
> benefit of the spectators – an absurd and crippling
> thing to do. Immediately, I changed my own view
> and felt that he was right. I congratulated him on his
> courage.
>
> Then the dream changed and I was holding a baby
> in my arms. We seemed to be in harmony with each
> other and everything we did was in accord with the
> rhythm of a tune I was singing. I had a sense of vigour
> and strength in the baby. (Peter Lomas, *True and False
> Experience*, Allen Lane, 1973, p. 101)

Let that be a parable of what is for most of us a long
process. The baby is his undeveloped inner self, which
needs nurturing and caring for if it is to grow. But in order
to give it the care and attention it needs, some of the energy
must be withdrawn from driving himself round and round
the track of life to satisfy other people's expectations.

This may sound like subversive talk, as though I am
recommending wholesale abandonment of going to work
and earning a living. Not a bit of it. Paid work on other
people's terms is essential for modern societies to function.
But its nature is changing. Less and less is it the be-all and
end-all of many people's lives. (Paradoxically, some who
do have jobs spend all their waking hours at work. That,

too, can become a headlong flight from inner life and more humane values.) I am not devaluing the importance of jobs defined by others. In fact for young adults, having to adapt to the needs of a job on other people's terms is an important phase in emerging from the egocentricity of the teenage years and discovering the big wide world. All I am doing is making a plea, especially to not-so-young adults, for being more in touch with your inner self, whether you have a paid job or not, so that at least some of what you do each week is an expression of that self and not just a reaction to demand.

Here is an exercise to help you to be more aware of the demands and expectations which dictate your daily activities.

AN EXERCISE

Take a large sheet of paper and some coloured felt-tip pens. First draw the figure of yourself. Then draw in the various people in your life who have expectations of you or make demands on you of one kind or another. They could be individuals, your wife or husband, granny, the dog, your boss; institutions like the bank or the union; they could be vaguer and less easy to pin-point, like 'people at work' or 'the neighbours'; or even less tangible still, like 'society', or God. Draw in a figure or a symbol that represents each of these demands or expectations, and in a balloon next to each write the typical wording in which the 'message' seems to come to you, for example 'pay up, or else'; 'be strong'; 'don't step out of line'; 'keep your nose to the grindstone'; 'care for me' and so on. Use whatever colours feel right to you.

You may want to write in what you feel like saying in reply.

If the idea of another drawing exercise fills you with horror, note that this time the drawing part is not essential. Any symbols will do for the demands made on you. Use solid objects if you like. But be sure to write down the 'message' in each case. That is the main point of the exercise.

However you decide to do it, the aim is to notice how much of what you do is directed or dictated by others, and

to be more aware of your feelings about this. I am not suggesting that you immediately go out and act upon your
feelings! That is a separate issue which needs conscious
choice, not indiscriminate acting out. But greater awareness
opens the way to more conscious choosing in your life.

ABOUT SCHOOL

He always wanted to say things, but no one understood.
He always wanted to explain things. But no one cared. So
he drew.

Sometimes he would just draw and it wasn't anything. He
   wanted to carve it in stone or write it in the sky.
He would lie out on the grass and look up in the sky and
   it would be only him and the sky and the things inside
   that needed saying.

And it was after that, that he drew the picture. It was a
   beautiful picture. He kept it under the pillow and would
   let no one see it.
And he would look at it every night and think about
   it. And when it was dark, and his eyes were closed, he
   could still see it.
And it was all of him. And he loved it.

When he started school he brought it with him. Not to
   show anyone, but just to have it with him like a friend.

It was funny about school.
He sat in a square, brown desk like all the other square,
   brown desks and he thought it should be red.
And his room was a square, brown room. Like all the other
   rooms.
And it was tight and close. And stiff.

He hated to hold the pencil and the chalk, with his arm
   stiff and his feet flat on the floor, with the teacher
   watching and watching.
And then he had to write numbers. And they weren't
   anything.
They were worse than the letters that could be something
   if you put them together.
And the numbers were tight and square and he hated the
   whole thing.

The teacher came and spoke to him. She told him to wear

a tie like all the other boys. He said he didn't like them and she said it didn't matter.

After that they drew. And he drew all yellow and it was the way he felt about morning. And it was beautiful.

The teacher came and smiled at him. 'What's this?' she said. 'Why don't you draw something like Ken's drawing? Isn't that beautiful?'

It was all questions.

After that his mother bought him a tie and he always drew airplanes and rocket ships like everyone else.

And he threw the old picture away.

And when he lay out alone looking at the sky, it was big and blue and all of everything, but he wasn't anymore.

He was square inside and brown, and his hands were stiff, and he was like anyone else. And the thing inside him that needed saying didn't need saying anymore.

It had stopped pushing. It was crushed. Stiff. Like everything else.

(quoted by Peter Lomas, *True and False Experience*, pp. 94–5)

3

Enquire Within

For many years now I have been running a course of ten weekly sessions called 'Journey Inward, Journey Outward'. It gives people the opportunity to see how the link between prayer and action might be strengthened in their life; and in particular to work with the question, 'What are my gifts and how is God calling me to use them at this point in my life?' One woman who came on the course a few years ago came because she felt she was involved with too many activities, Samaritans, church committees and a full-time teaching job, to say nothing of bringing up teenage children. She felt pulled many ways and wanted to see more clearly what she should be doing with her energies. At the end of the ten weeks she was not much clearer! But as the years passed it became plainer that her resistance to change was not in the fact that she was doing too many things. Her resistance was an internal one, a fear to look within. Her many activities were a way of avoiding that inner work.

The urge to search for the treasure is very strong and can exercise a great fascination. But instinctively we feel that the search could be fraught with risk. Our instinct is right on both counts: the treasure *is* supremely worth searching for; and the search always involves risk of one kind or another. Any children's adventure story recognises that, and the attraction of such stories lies in the fact that they are parables of a real live search. There lies within each of us a treasure chest covered in barnacles, half buried in silt, like an old box at the bottom of the sea that no one would look at twice. But inside is a very precious stone, that is to be brought out and shaped and polished: it is to be a gift to enrich others.

That is the image used in Revelation 2:17: 'I will give you a white stone, and on the stone will be written a new name, known to none but the one who receives it.' The new name is God's unique and personal name for you, the 'you' that you could be. The metaphor of the hidden treasure appears in Matthew 13:44: 'The kingdom of heaven is like treasure hidden in a field, which someone found and covered up; then in his joy he goes and sells all that he has and buys that field.' Like much of Jesus' teaching, this parable has an inner meaning as well. The treasure which is the kingdom is hidden within you. The supremely important thing in life is to search for it and bring it out: that is the one thing necessary, worth subordinating everything else to make it possible.

So, is the process of opening yourself to the calling of God a bit like a treasure hunt? Only in a rather rough and ready sense. In some ways the treasure image is too static. It is not simply a case of digging something up and putting it on view. In terms of this metaphor, you are only a treasure when you enrich others: you cease to be one when you hoard yourself. So the notion of the treasure has a dynamic connotation. It refers to what you *do*, or at least what you are for others. The poet Andrew Harvey put it neatly in a newspaper interview. The journalist had remarked that modern poetry struck him as self-indulgent. Harvey replied: 'You don't mind my saying this? Maybe you are putting off an engagement with your own self. Perhaps one definition of journalism is that the observer is always observing. But poetry demands the enactment of oneself. Then you have to face yourself in a very frightening way' (*Guardian*, 9 June 1984). Digging up your treasure means precisely the enactment of yourself. Calling or vocation in the sense I mean it arises at the three-way meeting between the person with her particular qualities, the needs of people in society, and God's nudging of things in the direction of the fulfilment that Christians call 'the kingdom'.

It must be said too that the word 'hunt' is not quite right either. It makes it sound more directional and active than it actually is, as though it is something you make a bee-line for. In some ways it is more a matter of noticing than of hunting; more sitting still and sharpening all your senses than rushing about with your nose to the ground like a dog who scents a rabbit. Searching for the treasure means opening your eyes and ears to your inmost longings and leanings, to the pain and impoverishment of people, and to God's dreams of what might be.

As I suggested in Chapter 1, one way of paying this kind of attention is to keep a notebook or loose-leaf binder in which you keep the work and the reflections prompted by the exercises this book is offering. This kind of jotting is sometimes called keeping a journal. 'Journal' makes it sound as though you have to be a writer. Not a bit of it! It is not meant for anyone else to read, and it certainly does not need to be spelt right. It does not even need to be all in words: you can include drawings and doodles, in fact anything that can be put on paper. Keeping a journal can be a valuable way of becoming more aware of your own life as a story, as a journey, as a voyage of discovery. If you want more ideas as to how you might keep a journal have a look at *At a Journal Workshop* by Ira Progoff, or attend a journal workshop yourself.

When they first start doing the kind of exercises I am offering, people often wonder if they are doing them right. Take for example the one in the last chapter. When I have offered it for a group to do, and we come to the point where people can share how they found it, one person may say, 'I'm afraid I have done it wrong, I drew myself in one corner of the sheet,' just because the other three people who have spoken drew themselves in the middle. The urge to conform, not to be different, 'to do it right', is often very strong. It is very important not to be ruled by this. After all, the treasure buried within you will not be a standard size and weight, like a package from a supermarket. There will be something unique about it, something non-standard, something unexpected, something that is not quite the same as anyone else that you have ever heard of. If you think you know what you are looking for, you are probably on the wrong track. So it is important to give up your assumptions, your wish 'to do it correctly', and your desire to be like everyone else.

It may help if you try to be a bit more aware of that part of you that insists 'mind you do it right'. At a day for Methodist ministers who wanted some help with learning to pray, we came to call this inner watchdog 'the parrot on my shoulder'. Many of us have an inner tyrant, critic, or judge sitting like a parrot on our shoulder. For some, an inner school-teacher is always telling you: 'This is the proper way to do it.' Or an inner accuser is quick to point out: 'You made a right mess of that.' For others the inner parrot will say flatly, 'You can't do that, you're not clever enough.'

The parrot I speak of is an inner voice, for example the voice that sometimes takes one part in an inner dialogue when you speak of 'wrestling with yourself', when you go over and over some incident in which you regret the part you played. You may not be aware of it as a voice; sometimes it is more like an implied opinion that carries weight within you. So, for example, going over an incident in your mind, you might find yourself working out what you wish you had said. The parrot may simply be the implied critic in your ruminations, the inner observer who hardly needs to say anything, because you immediately start justifying yourself without the parrot needing to say anything at all! Though it is an inner voice in the sense that I have tried to describe, it is often an amalgam of things parents or teachers have said. Sometimes it will be the mouthpiece of less easily identifiable influences, including some of the ones outlined in the last chapter.

It is possible that the parrot may be right on occasion. It is then appropriate to call it the voice of conscience. But very few of us grow to adulthood without our conscience needing to be educated and informed. Part of that process is becoming aware of what the parrot says and checking it against the facts and against your consciously evaluated moral code. But first you need to become aware of your particular parrot and its characteristics. If you like, you could draw in your parrot on the sheet that you used for the exercise in Chapter 2, together with some of its typical phrases.

One other point about the exercises. As you do them, be willing to let go of your urge to control what happens: that is an important disposition to cultivate in the search. For there is a sense in which you are not only searching for something: something is searching for you (see John Sanford, *The Kingdom Within*, 1970, p. 40). As St Matthew put it, 'The kingdom of heaven is like a merchant in search of fine pearls' (13:45). He has already said the kingdom is like buried treasure. In the next breath he likens it to a merchant searching. So it is important to allow yourself to be searched for, by the kingdom, by God, by the self that you could become. And to do that requires a letting go and a willingness to encounter surprises.

When the famous impresario Diaghilev was gathering around him in Paris a group of very talented people in the arts, Jean Cocteau, a young man in his twenties, was very keen to join them. He had the temerity to ask the great man if he could be part of the enterprise. Diaghilev replied tersely: 'Surprise me.' Surprise, the unexpected, is an essential aspect of creativeness. God, as the title of a book by Gerard W. Hughes reminds us, is a God of surprises. You may be sure that God's call to you to be creative, to discover and to exercise your particular gift, will involve some surprises too.

As you read this you might think to yourself, 'I have no particular gift. I'm not gifted. I'm just not a creative person.' A good example of parrot talk! I believe everyone has a gift, potentially. But I will not try to persuade you of this: all I ask for now is that you be willing to suspend judgment about it. Start taking the parrot talk a bit less seriously. Tell it to clear off; and be a bit more open to your hidden depths and to the whisperings and nudgings of God.

AN EXERCISE

Find somewhere where you can be quiet and undisturbed, provide yourself with pencil and paper, and set aside at least half an hour. Begin by being quiet: close your eyes, and for a minute or two just become aware of the sensations you experience in breathing. This will help you to let go of the immediate concerns and demands of your daily life and be more in touch with your inner stillness. After preparing yourself in this way, draw a clock face without putting the hands in.

Ask yourself: 'What time is it in my life?' Listen, as it were, for a time of day (or night) to suggest itself to you. If nothing comes, repeat the question to yourself and let your mind go blank for a few moments till a time suggests itself. This is not a reasoned process of working out the seasons of your life and trying to fit them logically to times of day: it is a matter of allowing a time to come into your mind. When it seems clear, draw in the hands at that time on the clock face. Then reflect about this: jot down your feelings about it being that time in your life.

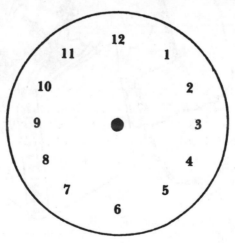

I have done this exercise myself a number of times. On each occasion the time on the clock face has been widely different. Here is what I wrote the first time I did it:

It's 5 p.m. A slight feeling of chill, at first; a lot of my life has gone. But, good heavens, it's 5 o'clock! I've finished with 9–5, working on other people's terms. I have the freedom now to work in my own way. I can use my time as I like; and yet sometimes even now I find myself structuring it again, renouncing the freedom I have. It is 5 p.m. I have a lot of experience and understanding of people now which I find great joy in offering to others.

I was forty-eight at the time and had just resigned from twenty-one years of full-time work as an Anglican vicar in order to start the Journey Inward, Journey Outward project.

If you find the exercise productive, you could use the following sentence-beginnings as a further stimulus to reflection. Complete each sentence a few times:

It's too late to . . .
It's too soon to . . .
It's the right time for . . .
I need time for . . .
I expect that . . . will happen at . . . o'clock.
An alarm is set for . . . o'clock. It means . . .

The best way is to write these quickly on the spur of the moment – the first things that come into your mind. Then jot down your feelings about what you have written. (This exercise originates from G. F. Simons, *Keeping Your Personal Journal*, Paulist Press, 1978, pp. 106–7.)

ANONYMOUS ANNUNCIATION

In the Royal Hotel, Woburn Place, A. L. Lloyd was lecturing about Romanian Folk Music. Round us were showcases containing examples of embroidered shirts and objects connected with music or agriculture. I had come alone, from Gray's Inn Road, in a state of mind that matched the weather: bleak, bone-chilling. I was in trouble and could see no way out, except by a miracle. I did not believe in that kind of a miracle. I had ceased to call myself a Christian, or a pacifist. My motives for being either – or rather, of trying to be either, for I had never quite succeeded: I had lived, as it were, on the legacy of a belief which I expected shortly to inherit – my motives now seemed insufficient. I had done the wrong thing all along the line, though (it seemed to me) I could not have chosen otherwise.

A. L. Lloyd was talking about the way, in Romania, folk songs had been passed from one generation to another. A mother (did he really say this, or do I imagine it?) would teach her daughter how to sing a song, saying: 'You don't see the point or meaning of this song now, but you will need it later.' As if she were giving her a magic spell or a bottle of medicine.

Suddenly I noticed that something was happening. I no longer felt alone and clue-less; or rather, I felt that being like this did not matter for, whatever happened, I was being lifted by a kind of tide or ocean: and not only I, but all the men and women and children, probably the dogs and cats and leaves as well if they had ever thought about it. Even if we were alone, we were all alone together. This offered a kind of courage: not hope, perhaps, but comradeship. And though my personal future still seemed like a dark and narrow tunnel which I must travel into without any promise of daylight at the other end, this prospect began to feel less like a death sentence from a doctor or a judge and more like a song.

Song, I saw, was the key: and folk song in particular. Here, for me at any rate, was the spell, the medicine, which I could not understand yet which could heal me all the same. It demanded no impossible belief in God or Jesus or the Virgin Birth; it demanded no political allegiance; it did

not seem to care if you were a monk or married, a com-
mando or a pacifist.

Still listening to A. L. Lloyd and looking at the corn-
dollies, I was trying to sort out this experience which I was
having. I wasn't even sure, in a way, that I was having it.
It was like a possibility I had caught sight of, out of the
corner of my eye: which might come closer, if I didn't
frighten it, and declare itself to me. Even eat out of my
hand (or feed me out of its hand: for it seemed a two-way
process).

Could this be God, creeping up on me after I had said
goodbye; after I had given up banging on his Christian
gateway? If so, the less I said about it the better, for the
moment anyway. The important thing was not to overstate
or understate: not to try to fit into any sort of category.
Above all, not to try to equate it with God, still less with
the name of Jesus. If I did (I knew) a kind of blight of
insincerity, of fear, of sentimentality, would spoil it all. So,
call it nothing: watch it, from the corner of an eye. (Sydney
Carter, *Dance in the Dark*, Collins, 1980, pp. 155–6)

4

Be Still and Know

There was once a man who had a very bad memory. It was so bad that when he got out of bed in the morning it took him an hour to get dressed because he could not remember where he had left his clothes. So he hit on the idea of writing a note to himself to say where he had put each garment as he undressed before going to bed. The next morning he got up and started looking for his shirt. He happened to stumble on the note on his bedside table and it said that his shirt was hanging in the wardrobe. He was overjoyed, and by using his list was able to dress in record time. Then he thought to himself, 'Now, where am I?' He consulted his note, but there was no answer.

Where are you? For a minute or two notice where you are. Look up from this page, and be aware of your surroundings, however familiar they may be. You may have sat down to read for a bit and perhaps do the exercise at the end of this section. I would like to suggest first a different exercise, that for the next fifteen minutes you lay this book aside and do nothing. Just sit comfortably and enjoy the peace of your room without feeling any obligation to do anything. Notice the colours, forms and textures of the things you can see. Be aware of sounds. Get up and stroll if you like, but if you do, move more slowly than you normally do, and let go of the desire to get somewhere. If you find yourself setting any kind of goal, however small, gently stop yourself; restrain your desire to achieve anything at all. This time is just for 'being', as though you were on holiday with no duties to attend to. If your parrot tells you you should be doing something useful, take no notice. Let go of all that, and enjoy this time. . . .

Now take a few minutes to jot down what you noticed in that brief holiday, what you noticed in your surroundings, but especially what you noticed about yourself, what passed through your mind. How easy was it to let go in this way? Did you think of all sorts of things that needed doing? Did you resist the temptation to rush off and do them? Did you feel guilty about doing nothing? Did you feel restless? Did you fall asleep? These questions are not meant to encourage you to pass judgment on yourself, simply to notice what happened.

I hope that you enjoyed that time, but if you found it quite a challenge, then that is not surprising. After all, we live in a very activist world, where action, success and achievement are overvalued to the exclusion of this other dimension of life. Douglas Steere calls this activism and over-work 'a pervasive form of contemporary violence'. He writes:

> to allow oneself to be carried away by a multitude of conflicting concerns, to surrender to too many demands, to commit oneself to too many projects, to want to help everyone in everything, is to succumb to violence . . . The frenzy of the activist neutralizes his work for peace . . . It destroys the fruitfulness of his own work, because it kills the root of inner wisdom which makes work fruitful. (quoted in Thomas Merton, *Conjectures of a Guilty Bystander*, Sheldon Press, 2nd edn 1977, p. 83)

That last sentence is the nub of the matter. If our action is to grow more and more from what we most deeply are and can be, then it needs to spring from an inner silence and stillness. I cannot prove this to you, I can only appeal to such hints and glimpses of this truth that you may already have, and encourage you to give more attention to them and to build more 'space' into your life. *To do this you may have to be very determined indeed.* You will not only have to contend with the contrary assumptions of people round you, like the admiration that is often accorded to 'selfless' people who busy themselves with kindly activity all day and every day. You will also have to contend with your own inner fifth column, the representative of that kind of opinion within you.

If you manage to make some headway against these two, there remains a third factor to contend with, which is the strongest of all, and that is your own underlying fear. Sooner or later in your journey into silence you will encounter fear, fear of inactivity, fear of being useless, fear of nothingness, fear of annihilation, nameless fears, formless fears. You may be aware of it quite quickly. For some, silence in a group of people engenders fear. Even in a prayer group, say, when there is a time of silence, a person may find herself becoming tense and involuntarily tightening against something, she knows not what. For others it is silence in solitude that brings fear to the surface, and any excuse will do to get up and do something. It may make itself felt first in the form of boredom, which is often a shield the mind manufactures to keep fear at bay. The fact is that any engagement with silence brings you more face to face with yourself.

Martin Israel says somewhere, 'God is eternally present; it is we who are so seldom at home in ourselves to receive him.' I like that, especially the implied hope that some day I might be at home in myself. It conjures up the picture of myself as a large house. Most of the time I live in the daytime rooms. There is also a room that I enter when I sleep. There are attics and cellars, parts of the house that I rarely visit, parts of it where the door has not been opened for years and the key has been lost, parts that have been walled up, the existence of which I am unaware. It may not sound very attractive to you. What I like about it is the hope that it implies, against all appearances to the contrary, that the whole of this house that I am could be home, that I could feel settled and at home in every part of it. That is to me a very attractive hope, the hope of wholeness, the hope of the inclusion and integration of all that I am; and the hope too that I can be open and hospitable to God's presence in every room, that it could be God's house.

But of course the way to that wholeness means coming to terms with all sorts of unacceptable aspects of my nature and my history. We will come back to this later. For now, suffice it to say that engaging with silence can begin to raise some of these things. I say this, not to put you off but to encourage you that it is to be expected. You may find that your first experiences with deliberate silence and stillness are wonderful. You may feel bathed in contentment and thoroughly refreshed, and if that is so, it is to be greatly welcomed. But do not be dismayed if it does not continue, and above all do not give up. Sooner or later making space for silence has to become a matter for discipline, not just in order to contend with outer opinions but also because you will encounter inner resistances, not least the barrage of distractions that will assail your mind.

It is not my intention to say a lot about this. There are now fortunately many books offering advice on silence and stillness as a method of prayer. Here I simply want to encourage you to do two things. One is to begin to make space for this in your own life, if you do not already do so. The other is to be inventive and resourceful about it.

The most winsome and attractive description of how to set about building some stillness into your life is to be found in Metropolitan Anthony of Sourozh's *School for Prayer* (DLT, 1970 and 1999). He describes how, soon after his ordination, an old lady came and asked his advice about prayer. She complained that in spite of praying the Jesus prayer (this consists of repeating the words 'Lord Jesus Christ have mercy on me' as a kind of mantra) for fourteen years, she was never aware of God's presence. He tells her to go to her room after breakfast, light her candle before her icon and sit herself down to knit. But he forbids her to say a word of prayer: 'You just sit and enjoy the peace of your room.' She does, and the first thing that strikes her is the pleasure of doing nothing for fifteen minutes without feeling guilty. Then he describes how she becomes aware of the silence, and that the silence is not so much absence of something but presence of something, and how at times in this way she begins to be aware of God's presence, even if only for a few moments at a time. Metropolitan Anthony describes this in a self-deprecating and apparently artless way. In fact it is an extremely artful description of one method of entering into silence, starting from the need to desist from activity, and moving on to the eventual necessity for some equivalent of knitting, that is, an undemanding focus which will gently hold your attention in the present. I will be offering some suggestions for this in the exercise at the end of this chapter.

What Metropolitan Anthony is describing is the process of becoming present. What that means is easiest to explain with reference to what it is not: it is not 'being miles away'. There are three ways of being miles away. One is remembering, going off into the past, going over in your mind things that happened an hour ago or last week. Another is anticipating, going off into the future, looking forward to, planning, or dreading things that are going to happen; or daydreaming about things that might happen. A third is thinking. A friend was wanting to learn how to be present. To help her begin to understand what it meant I asked her to choose an object to focus her attention on. She chose one of the armchairs in the room where we were meeting. I suggested she noticed as much as she could about that old chair, its shape, colour and texture, as though she was going to draw it. She was silent for a time. After a few minutes I asked her to describe what she had noticed. She described some features of the chair and then said she started thinking about all the people who might have sat in that chair. That is an example of thinking. There is nothing wrong with it in its place; and it may be very edifying to look at, say, a candle and reflect on Jesus as the light of the world and how you also are to be a light to people. But it is not being present. And the *basic* requirement of prayer is being present, even if that conscious focus is only used at the beginning of the time of prayer.

So far it may have seemed that I have slid from talking about 'being' to talking about focused times of prayer. What I want to convey is that the two overlap, in the sense that at its most basic prayer *is* being present; it is being here as opposed to being miles away. That after all is the prerequisite for any genuine relatedness. Prayer, as a part of your relationship with God, is the time you spend consciously or intentionally with God. From the human side what that requires at the very least is the attempt to be present, just as in a relationship between two people times of being present to one another are essential. What proportion of your prayer time you spend in this way will vary with different temperaments. For one it might be a brief time of centring at the start; for another it might occupy most of their prayer time. In no sense is this book intended as an exposition of all the different kinds of prayer. I simply want to make a plea for a place for some receptiveness and listening in prayer, because that is an essential part of the process of being open to God's calling.

But if you are to have focused times of prayer, of being present to God, you will need to make other kinds of space in your life, less formal, more haphazard times of free-wheeling, of letting go, of playing. Thomas Merton, talking about distractions in prayer, writes: 'It is no good trying to clear your mind ... at the moment of meditation, if you do nothing to cut down the pressure of work outside that time' (*Seeds of Contemplation*, 1972, p. 173). For many people, expecting to start with a daily time of silence or stillness may be trying to run before you can walk. I think for example of a vicar's wife in a housing estate parish who felt that in their busy vicarage there were so many pressures upon her, expectations from her husband and from the parishioners, that it was impossible for her even to think of having times of stillness at home. She needed to get away completely, perhaps for a day a month, to some place of quiet and tranquillity to begin to make some sort of space in her life for *her*. For another person, taking the dog out is a time of free-wheeling and the starting point where he begins to discover what 'being' might be. So you may need to be quite inventive, as well as determined, in beginning to make space for being in your life. But if you are going to be serious about your relatedness with God you will discover sooner or later the need for more clearly focused times of being present.

One of my interests as a parish priest was in counselling. Quite early on I discovered that one of the most important things for a counsellor to learn is to be willing to feel useless, to be apparently unable to be of help to someone and yet to be willing to go on listening to them. Any pastor or counsellor who has not learned that can be a menace! It is not the only important quality for a pastor, but in my view it is high on the list. So with prayer one of the first things to discover is that it is not about achieving or effecting or acquiring something. That is quite difficult to realise in a world which overvalues achievement and action. Even reminding people that prayer is basically the expression of a relationship is not necessarily an antidote for a generation raised on a diet of TV soap-operas, where relatedness is seen primarily in terms of power struggles and manipulation.

It took me more than three decades to begin to realise that prayer might have more to do with being than with striving. I could blame people like my teachers in theological college for perpetuating my myopia. As I remember it, we had endless lectures on dryness in prayer, which was our only encouragement for a mandatory hour and a half in chapel before breakfast every morning. Prayer was presented to us as an unremitting grind in which feelings were out of place. For me it only endorsed what had already been impressed on me by my elders and betters, that the business of being a Christian was about duty and striving to be good.

It was not until years after my ordination that I began to realise that God might be loving and accepting and not some kind of slave-driver in the sky. When I moved to my second curacy it was a very go-ahead parish by the standards of the day. We used to have house communions on weekdays when a group of churchgoers from a neighbourhood would gather in the sitting-room of a council house for an early morning Eucharist before work. The custom was to sit for the service. I was glad to go along with that at that hour, but when it came to receiving communion I was the only one who knelt. It felt irreverent not to. I must have seemed an awful prig. After a few months I began to feel, 'Well, if you can't beat 'em, join 'em.' I began to sit to receive communion. A bit of me half expected thunderbolts from heaven, but none came. In fact it began to dawn on me that maybe God was not the taskmaster I thought he was; that I did not have to earn his acceptance by striving and struggle; that what he had to give was free and without conditions; and all I had to do was to hold out my hands to receive it. I should add that it was at least another ten years before that slow dawning began to become daylight. I mention this to illustrate how slow and difficult it can be to move away from a striving, effortful attitude to one that is more relaxed and receptive.

The other day, in conversation with someone who came to talk about the direction of his life, the subject of prayer and silence and 'being' came up, as it usually does sooner or later. He told me that he did not have any daily time of prayer, but one evening a week he met others in church for a time of silence. I thought that sounded as though it could be quite a help to him. But it transpired that it was an intercession group to pray for the parish. It was not, as he put it, for his benefit but for others. Rather wistfully he asked, 'Wouldn't it be selfish and self-indulgent if it was for me?' I hope that, from what I am trying to say, you will understand that it is not 'selfish' or 'self-indulgent' to stop driving yourself occasionally and put yourself in the way of receiving. On the contrary, it is essential if you are genuinely to become a gift to others.

The title of this chapter is a quotation from Psalm 46. 'Let be', says the Hebrew version, 'and know that I am God.' The Greek one has: 'Have leisure, and know that I am God.' Perhaps the ancients understood this better than we do.

AN EXERCISE

This is offered in two forms, both of which are for practising being present; one is more free-wheeling, the other more disciplined. You might like to try them both.

1. Take a walk on your own somewhere reasonably quiet, in the country or in a park. Walk more slowly than you normally would, and as you walk notice as much as you can of what you can see and hear. Stop frequently to listen, to the song of a bird or to other sounds. Stop to look; notice the detail in the bark of a tree or the leaves of a bush or the stonework of a wall. Open your eyes and your ears as wide as you can, take time to be more aware of your surroundings in all their detail and their variety.

When you have finished your walk, sit quietly for a time to let your inner silence take root a little.

2. Find a place where you can be uninterrupted. If necessary, arrange for the family not to disturb you for whatever length of time you choose. Sit in an upright chair, with a cushion if it is too low, or a book under your feet if it is too high, so that the upper part of your legs is parallel with the floor. Better still, use one of those orthopaedic chairs that support both your knees and your bottom in a half-sitting, half-kneeling position. Hold your spine and head erect, with your hands loosely on your lap or your thighs. Let your mind become quiet and still; be content just to be. If there are any particular worries or concerns that tug at your attention, give them to God for these minutes, for him to take care of. If it helps jot the most insistent ones on a piece of paper and deliberately put it to one side for this time. Then use one of the following devices for helping you to be present:

i) With your eyes closed, be aware of the sounds you can hear. Just listen to them each in turn noticing as much as you can about the sound itself, its quality, its tone, its variation, and so on. Do not think *about* them or wonder what is making them. Simply give your attention to the actual sounds. Let them be the focus to keep you in the present. Do not be hard on yourself if your mind wanders: just bring it gently back by focusing on the sounds you can hear.

ii) With eyes closed, be aware of the sensations in the various parts of your body in turn, your left foot, lower left leg, upper left leg, right foot, lower right leg, upper right leg, buttocks, lower trunk, chest, back, shoulders, left hand, left arm, right hand, right arm, neck, face and head. Then briefly be aware of the sensations of your whole body as you sit quietly. And then do the rounds again from your toes to the crown of your head, briefly pausing to give attention to each part. And so on. The aim is not to *change* the sensations, but to be more aware of them; the aim is not primarily relaxation but awareness. If you feel more relaxed afterwards, that is a by-product.

iii) With eyes open, choose an object to look at as the focus of your attention. It need not be interesting or attractive, just something to hold your attention. Become as aware as you can of its shape, colour, texture, and so on. If you find your mind going off into interesting thoughts about it, bring it gently back to observing it. Look at it as though you were going to draw it.

iv) Find a suitable small object to hold in your hand. Let your awareness of the sensations of holding it be the focus to keep your attention in the present.

Those are four devices for helping you to be present. There are others, for example using your breathing as a focus (that is, simple physical awareness of the sensations of breathing), but these will do to start with. Choose the one you find easiest: there is no need to make it needlessly difficult for yourself! You will need to persevere with it, even through times when it feels impossible. Do not worry if your mind wanders. It will. Just bring your attention gently back and be here.

You may or may not be aware of God's presence as you

do this. No matter. Be assured that God is here: and when you are here, you are always in God's presence, whether you are aware of it or not.

(If you want to pursue this process further, there is a tape which you may find helpful, available from the address on p. 207. Also, Anthony de Mello, *Sadhana: A Way to God*, 1978, is a useful DIY book.)

THE RAINMAKER

In a remote village in China a long drought had parched the fields, the harvest was in danger of being lost and the people were facing starvation in the months to come. The villagers did everything they could. They prayed to their ancestors; their priests took the images from the temples and marched them round the stricken fields, but no ritual and no prayers brought rain.

In despair they sent far afield for a 'Rainmaker'. When the little old man arrived they asked him if there was anything he needed. He replied, 'Nothing, only a quiet place where I can be alone.' They gave him a little house and there he lived, quietly doing the things one has to do in life, and on the third day the rain came. (Irene Claremont de Castillejo, *Knowing Woman*, Harper and Row, 1974, p. 133)

The writer who tells this story comments that the Rainmaker does not cause the rain to come: he allows it; that is to say, he does not prevent it.

5

Know God

'The most beautiful thing which a person can say about God would be for that person to remain silent from the wisdom of an inner wealth. So, be silent, and stop flapping your gums about God' (Matthew Fox, *Meditations with Meister Eckhart*, 1983, p. 44). Meister Eckhart's quaint advice needs to be heeded in these days of fundamentalism and zealotry. In this chapter I shall be saying more about the images and notions that stand in the way of knowing God, than claiming to know the unknowable.

On 6 July 1984 David Jenkins was consecrated bishop in York Minster. Three days later the south transept of the minster was struck by lightning. The bishop's critics claimed that this was proof that God was on their side. (Someone else commented that if it was a thunderbolt from God he wasn't a very good shot!) The event had evidently stirred murky depths in our communal psyche. I remember reading an article about the fire at the time by an atheist journalist who confessed to slight shivers down the spine. It sounded as though it had stirred up an atavistic and primitive notion of God in the mind of someone who with his reason professed disbelief. I sometimes wonder whether, because this age has largely let slip the more conscious and explicit awareness of God, the notion of God in our collective consciousness has sunk back to a more primeval level, from which it sometimes gets activated in a vindictive and tyrannical form. I am of course speaking of our notion of God, our mental image, not of God as s/he is.

That journalist needed to be an atheist. Anyone whose idea of God is that vengeful needs to be an atheist for his own self-preservation! There are many Christians who labour under notions almost as heavy. In my experience, negative notions of God are much commoner among church people than one might hope.

Sometimes at a conference or workshop I offer people the opportunity to notice the main negative component in their idea of God. The easiest way into this is to remember how you thought of God when you were a child. I ask them to draw how they thought of God. One person might draw an eye or eyes looking down at her, all-seeing like T. S. Eliot's railway cat who 'will watch you without winking and he sees what you are thinking, and it's certain he doesn't approve of hilarity and riot'; a kind of celestial observer with a critical eye, who misses nothing. Another will draw a judge, like Joan Brockelsby's 'faces intent upon decision, stern, concentrated, hard in the eye, red in the face, cold, cold in the thinking', holding scales like the figure of Justice on top of the Old Bailey in London. One man, who as a child had been told that God would 'get him' if he did not do as he was told, drew a straight road leading up to the gate of heaven with the caption: 'You must keep to the straight and narrow, OR ELSE!' Another draws someone sitting in an armchair, resolutely behind the paper while a child holding a toy car stands mutely by knowing that he is not worth any attention. When I show a few illustrations like this to stimulate people's reflection, I usually include one of a bearded old gent in the clouds. You might think that is not a negative image. But even positive images can stand in the way. A friend who had a very good relationship with her father when she was young was for many years after her father's death unaware that she thought of God in the image of her father. It was quite a shock to her to discover that her conception of God completely excluded God's 'otherness', what you might call God's trans-human qualities.

When I was about nine I found a ten-shilling note in the road, unimaginable riches for a small boy at that time. I particularly remember my father's comment: 'That will be a reward for some good deed you have done.' My parents believed that you never got anything for nothing, and this was elevated to the status of a moral principle: 'You should not get anything for nothing.' It was not until years later that I began to realise how this had coloured my view of God. As I said in the last chapter, I always thought God's love and acceptance had to be earned by effort and hard work; it never crossed my mind that it was given free, gratis and for nothing. So experiences from the past and the attitudes of our parents can colour, if not skew or even blot out, our view of God.

Sometimes it is not so clear that the origin is in our experience of our parents. I think of a divorced woman who had great difficulty with prayer and with any contact with God. When she pictured Jesus she imagined him with the same hypercritical qualities that her ex-husband had. Trying to relate to Jesus was obviously a non-starter for her. She needed to find a different approach to God to bypass all that, at least to start with. In one of our conversations she timidly mentioned that as a child she had always been aware of God in the presence of the reserved sacrament. (In some churches consecrated bread and wine from Holy Communion is kept for the communion of the sick or as an aid to devotion.) But she felt it was a bit childish for an adult to need that kind of prop. In fact it proved a very helpful way for her to begin to discover God's love for her.

All this could be summed up in the word projection. We commonly project upon God ideas or notions that say more about us than they do about God. It is frequently like that with comments about the weather. Have you noticed how they often say more about the speaker's mood than they do about what the weather has actually been like?

How then can any of us see beyond these spectres which

our mind by stealth constructs from our past? How can we know or even suspect their deception?

There are two ways, and for many of us both are necessary sooner or later. The first is that there is a relatively objective check provided by the scriptures. For Christians these are the Old and New Testaments. Here you can trace the gradual revelation of the nature of God, or people's gradual comprehension of God's nature, whichever way you prefer to look at it. For example, a quick glance through the Bible reveals a God who is creative and unexpectedly true to promises (Genesis). God's power is awesome and mysterious (Exodus). God is against oppressors and on the side of the poor (Amos); loving and patient (Hosea); vulnerable (the Gospels). God brings new life out of the most hopeless situations through the most improbable and apparently unsuitable people. These qualities gradually became apparent over many centuries. They may look contradictory: but each fills out and qualifies the others, without negating them. In other words God is God, not just a product of escapist fantasy or diseased conscience.

You may say that that kind of evidence is not objective: it is not independent of people's apprehension of it. If you are looking for that kind of objectivity about God, sufficient for watertight conviction, you will not find it in the Bible or any other religious tradition. The objectivity I speak of is the confirmation of a point of view over a long period by a lot of people's experience. That may not be intellectually compelling, and it is perfectly proper to question it, but it is far from valueless. If you are a person who questions everything though, beware of letting that be a barrier to living. Sooner or later you have to take the plunge and risk being wrong!

The second way of learning to look past our individual mental constructs of God's nature is to work at it from inside ourselves, as it were, to take the time and trouble to become more aware of our projections. This means getting counselling of some kind from someone who will help us to be more aware of how the hurts, grievances and frights of the past, and especially from our childhood, go on affecting us until we are willing to face them and integrate them. At some time or another most of us need someone who will accept us and listen to us deeply and attentively enough so that we can come to know what we feel about ourselves, about our parents and about our past; so that pent-up feelings can be discharged and we can be freer to live more in the present. If we are sincere in our search for God, most of us sooner or later encounter our need for this.

Here is an exercise to help you to be more aware of the images or notions that stand between you and God as s/he is.

TWO EXERCISES

1. Draw how you thought of God as a child: put yourself in the picture too. I did this for myself recently. It was very rough and ready; I am no artist and I did it in half a minute. I drew God as though he was saying, 'Do as you are told' and myself walking away, as though on an errand, a stooping, cringing shape, the unwilling slave I felt I used to be.

One person I showed it to remarked that it looked as though God was sending me away, which reminded me that I had felt that too, at one time. I suddenly felt a great pity and compassion for that poor little lad.

So drawing can express much more than words. Try it. Do not be too cautious and careful about the lines; let your hand rough it out quickly. You are not obliged to show it to anyone. And when you have done it, put your hand over the God part of it, and remember that in reality God deeply loves the little one you have drawn however unappealing he or she may appear to you.

2. If you wish, you could do something which will help you to focus on your present feelings about God. You will need a fist-sized lump of clay for this. Close your eyes and start randomly squeezing and squidging the clay. . . . After a minute or two, open your eyes. Does it remind you of anything . . . ? If so, make it more like that thing. . . . Reflect on it: does it have anything to say to you about how you are with God at present? . . .

If you cannot see anything in it, then close your eyes and try the process again . . . until it seems to remind you of something. . . .

Note that this is not about making something, but allowing the clay to bring something about how you are with God into your clearer awareness.

You may want to keep your piece of clay by you for a few days, so that you have a chance to absorb what it has raised for you.

FRED

'Fred' was considered a model Christian. He was young, married, and in addition to his professional work belonged to several voluntary bodies, took an intelligent interest in theology, lived a simple lifestyle, rarely dining out or going to films or theatre, and he and his wife spent most of their holiday time at conferences. On one of his holidays he came to make an individually given retreat. I encouraged him to pray by using his imagination on scenes from the gospel, entering the scene as though it were now happening and himself a participant. At the end of each day he would tell me what he had experienced in these scenes. One day he had been imagining the marriage feast at Cana. He had a vivid imagination and had seen tables heaped with food set out beneath a blue sky. The guests were dancing and it was a scene of great merriment. 'Did you see Christ?' I asked. 'Yes,' he said, 'Christ was sitting upright on a straight-backed chair, clothed in a white robe, a staff in his hand, a crown of thorns on his head, looking disapproving.'

Before praying this Cana scene, if he had been asked 'What is your basic notion of God and of Christ?', he would probably have answered, 'God is the God of love, mercy and compassion.' Deep down in his subconscious another image of God was effectively operating and influencing his life. As he reflected on this image of the disapproving Christ he began to understand many things in his own life. He saw a Christ who disapproved of merriment, who demanded an unceasing application to 'good works', a tyrannical Christ who did not permit the simple pleasures of life. He began to realize that he had never allowed himself to admit the truth that he really experienced no joy in his multiple commitments to good works. He felt constantly guilty and driven by an inexorable God. (Gerard W. Hughes, *God of Surprises*, DLT, 1985 and 1996, pp. 36–7)

What Might it Mean to Follow Christ?

A favourite hymn at carol services is 'Once in royal David's city'. Verse 3 always seems to me to be a rather blatant example of the attempt to use Christianity as an instrument of social control: 'Christian children all must be mild, obedient, good as he.' When it is a school carol service, the inclusion or omission of that verse might tell you a lot about the staff's attitudes to the children.

When I was young I thought this was what obedience to God meant, doing as you were told. Many Christian adults still think it means that. Some think it ought to mean that. But – I wonder. Is that really all it means? Or could it sometimes mean something more like obedience to the deepest laws of your own God-given nature?

In my better moments I think it could. But there have been many features of the way Christianity has been presented that have made it difficult to see that. I certainly grew up with the notion that we were to model our lives on that of Jesus. We were to subdue our own selves and our own desires and to 'put on Christ'. To someone of my temperament this sounded very like 'become a pale imitation of Christ', as though we were being told to ape his attitudes in a cardboard cut-out kind of way. We were, it seemed, to use up much of our energy suppressing our own impulses and to devote what strength remained to modelling ourselves on Christ. It made for a somewhat bloodless form of Christianity: most of the vitality was used up in self-squashing.

I have come to believe that following Christ can mean something more than this, something altogether more full-blooded and less life-denying. It is not that I do not think St Paul was right in pointing to all sorts of unruly and destructive desires within us. It is that I do not think that they are the last word about human nature. I believe that beneath and behind them lie tremendous capacities for love and for lively activity. It is a matter of digging deep enough to uncover the springs of our energy, and of not being seduced by our more superficial impulses. Elizabeth O'Connor says: 'We ask to know the will of God without guessing that his will is written into our very beings.' For my part I never dreamt that God's will could possibly coincide with anything I wanted. It never occurred to me that since s/he created me God's will might go very much *with* the grain of my being. What joy if that were true! What a release of energy and liveliness it would bring to people! How much more we would embody a gospel of *good* news!

There are other similar features about the way Christianity has been presented that have also conspired to obscure this truth. In the tradition in which I was brought up, for example, there was much emphasis on self-denial. We were taught that the cross is an 'I' with a line through it. No doubt teachers congratulated themselves on having devised this simple formula, easily understood by children, for explaining the practical meaning of the cross and the importance of self-denial. The trouble is, it did not take account of a child's stage of development. When it is addressed to mature adults it is very appropriate, if a developed awareness of their gifts can be assumed. For example, when self-denial is enjoined upon a teacher it *assumes* that you are generous with your teaching ability, that you give your all in the classroom; and it adds 'but do not impose yourself upon your pupils, do not use them for your own self-gratification, and when it is appropriate take a back seat and let them shine'.

But if you tell a *child* to exercise self-denial, there is a danger of conveying quite a different message. A child's identity, selfhood and gifts are undeveloped. They cannot in any real sense give a self they have not yet become. That is after all why the law forbids the marriage of under-age young people. So for a child the giving of self which provides the context for self-denial is impossible except in a very undeveloped way. 'Deny yourself' easily comes across as 'stop your identity developing'; it becomes a useful tool for bringing children into line. When that happens the gospel flies out of the window.

Before trying to describe what it might mean to follow Christ in the light of these reflections, let me mention two other factors that have tended to reinforce what you might call the across-the-grain view. The first is another feature of the way Christianity is presented. There is often much emphasis on the cross. That is of course appropriate: the cross is after all not only a pivotal doctrine of the Christian faith but also the one that distinguishes it from all other world religions. But this emphasis can give a misleading impression. To hear some Christian preachers you would think that the cross came at the *beginning* of Jesus' ministry instead of at the end. But if there is over-emphasis on the cross, if Christianity is defined as 'carrying your cross', it can sound like a formula for self-killing rather than self-giving.

The second factor has a secular origin. It is the notion that goodness or virtue is measured by the hardness or difficulty of a course of action; that unless you find an action hard or difficult or demanding it cannot really be called virtuous at all. This view has had a long innings in the history of philosophy and goes back at least as far as Antisthenes the Cynic who was a discipline of Socrates in the fifth century BC. If true, it would chop off at the knees any notion that going with the grain of your inmost being might be thought of as good or virtuous or moral. It would put it out of court as making virtue too easy. But for all its impressive supporters, I venture to question it. In doing so

I take comfort from the ironic words of the German poet
Schiller (1759–1805):

> How gladly I'd serve my friends, but alas,
>   I do so with pleasure.
> And so I have a nagging feeling that
>   it's unethical.

What then might following Christ mean? Some years ago
Dennis Potter's play *Son of Man* was broadcast on television. I was not able to see the whole play; but I have a
vivid recollection of Colin Blakely as Jesus stumbling
around in the desert full of angst and solitary self-doubt:
'Is it me? Am I the Messiah? What sort of Messiah? Wonder
worker? Powerful world ruler? Insulated from suffering?'
It was Dennis Potter's evocation of Jesus' temptation in
the wilderness – a mid-twentieth-century person looking
back down the centuries at the figure of Jesus and seeing
the reflection of his own face. But it set me thinking, not
least because I too am a child of this century. It rang some
bells with my own search for meaning and direction: what
was my next step in life to be? If Jesus too had to wrestle
with uncertainty, it gave me a sense of fellow-feeling with
him. Somehow it made him feel less far removed from my
own life.

As I reflected about this I was aware that if ordinary
human beings are to push the boat out, if we are to take
some new initiative, some new direction, most of us need
affirmation from somewhere. We need a basic inner knowledge that we are OK, that we are loved. Did Jesus have
that, or did he live on some higher plane, capable of doing
without such creaturely props? Well, no, apparently he did
not. At his baptism, at the very outset of his ministry, he
had precisely that kind of affirmation in the voice from
heaven: 'You are my son, my beloved, I delight in you,' as
St Mark has it. This expressed for Jesus that total love and
acceptance a child receives from a parent because he is his
child and not because of anything he has done or achieved.
(In my view 'I delight in you' represents the meaning of
the Greek more accurately than 'in whom I am well

pleased' which always sounds to me like a school report –
'has done pleasing work this term' – and has all the wrong
overtones.) I like to think that whenever Jesus went apart
to pray and to spend time alone with his Father, that he
heard again those lovingly affirmative words. In fact at the
transfiguration (Mark 9:7) they are again explicitly referred
to.

So it seemed to me there was some parallelism between
our life and Jesus' life. I began to look for more. I have
already begun to suggest in these pages that for each of us
our offering to the life of the world will be in the exercising
of our gifts. Could that in any sense be true of Jesus? Was
his ministry in any sense an exercising of his gifts? Could
any of what he did be seen as going with the grain of his
nature and natural aptitudes, or did the cross cast such a
dark shadow back over his life as to deny any validity to
that possibility? I for one do not think that it did. Jesus'
most obvious gift was for teaching. He was perhaps the
greatest teacher the world has seen. He used every possible
situation as a vehicle for putting over his message. In his
ministry in Galilee it would not be an exaggeration to say
that he was having the time of his life exercising his gift
as a teacher. It was the fact that he exercised his gift with
such freedom and generosity that aroused the fear and
envy of the authorities, which in the end brought him to
the cross. But in the earlier part of his ministry as Luke
presents it, though Jesus did begin quite soon to encounter
opposition from the authorities, they were powerless to do
anything because of his popularity. This prompts me to
look again at our life and to ask: If a person is having a
whale of a time exercising her gift with freedom, does it
ever happen that this arouses envy and fear in others? And
do these feelings sometimes lead people to try and obstruct
or push aside such a person in one way or another? I am
afraid it happens often, and it is one way in which we
must expect to encounter the cross.

These reflections have led me to set out in the table on
p. 54 what seem to me to be some parallelisms between
our life and the life of Christ. I have added two columns

which I have not mentioned yet. The first needs no explanation as we have already begun to look beyond 'oughts' and 'shoulds'; the fourth column sets out Jesus' call, what he was commissioned or called to do. I like to think of that as God's call to the whole Church. None of us as individuals is called to all of that, but we are each called to some tiny part of it. We will have more to say about this in Chapter 13. There are two other small points. First, each stage is not passed through once and for all but may be encountered or recapitulated many times. Secondly you can look at the process described as a long-term one, or in miniature. You can see it as a lifelong process; or you can pass through all these 'stages' in some measure in an hour or two.

This table, as I hope I have made clear, is not meant to be an exhaustive setting forth of the life and ministry of Jesus. Perhaps it is no more than seeing the reflection of our own faces. Does that sound an inappropriate thing to do? If *all* I see is the reflection of my own face, it probably is. But I believe I see more than that. I seem to discern the movements of a life that illuminate the movements of my own life. Episodes in the life of *the* son of God help to make sense of episodes in the life of any son or daughter of God. At least, I find that to be true in my experience.

So following Christ does not mean slavish imitation. It does not mean modelling yourself on some static, unchanging norm. It is more subtle than that. I believe we can expect broadly two movements in our following of Christ, just as there were two movements in his life – growth and diminishment, becoming and giving, the development of our gifts and the lavish expenditure of them at God's invitation, the exuberant giving of what we are and the acceptance of the pain that it will sometimes bring upon us.

Teilhard de Chardin identifies these two movements in *Le Milieu Divin*, and points out that books about the spiritual life do not generally give enough attention to the first, that of growth or becoming. He was writing in 1957: and

THE LIFE OF JESUS

Growing up	Baptism	Temptation in the desert	The commission	Ministry in Galilee	
Jesus aged 12 in the temple. Beginning the process of leaving his parents to be 'about his Father's business' (Luke 2:41-52)	'You are my son, my beloved: I delight in you' (Mark 1:11)	What kind of Son of God am I to be? Wonder worker? Powerful world ruler? Insulated from suffering? (Luke 4:1-13)	The Spirit of the Lord is upon me, to bring good news to the poor, release for prisoners, sight to the blind, freedom for the oppressed (Luke 4:18)	Having the time of his life exercising his gift of teaching (Luke 4:14-9:50)	'He set his face to go to Jerusalem' He faced the backlash, motivated by envy and fear 'He gave his back to the smiters' They killed him (Luke 9:51)

OUR LIFE

Growing up	Experience of the love and acceptance of God	The desert search	God's call to you	Giving what you've got	Meeting the cross
We need to leave our 'parents' – the 'oughts', 'shoulds' and 'musts' – to discover God's way for us	'You are my daughter, my beloved: you are my son, my beloved: I delight in you'	What is your life for? What is the treasure hidden within you that God calls out from you? What is to be your unique contribution to the life of the world at this stage in your life?	The Spirit of the Lord is upon you, to exercise your specific gift in some way to bring good news to the impoverished, or release for the imprisoned, or sight for the blinded, or freedom for the oppressed	Having a whale of a time exercising your gift	What you do for the kingdom will threaten vested interests Those who have not found what they're for will be envious You may die, e.g. to your reputation, status, comfort, friends, etc.

some more recent books do give expression to that. But their message, though accepted by many intellectually, is not widely lived in our church congregations. The fact is that there are considerable resistances in many of us to becoming aware of our gifts. Even that modest step in the direction of the kingdom can be difficult and costly, at least in prospect. It is after all much more comfortable to remain safely and cosily part of the anonymous crowd.

However, the two phases of the Christian life are not totally distinct or separate. We do not complete one and then go on to the other. They are very much intertwined. Both are important. If the growth phase is obscured we are left with a pallid life-denying obsession with death. If the diminishment phase is obscured we are left with a kind of gospel of the 'me' generation – 'do what you like; the very fact that you want to do something means it *must* be God's will'. So just as growth and diminishment both had a part to play in Jesus' life, we must expect both in our own life. Following Christ means becoming and then giving what we are, just as he became and gave what he was. As Sydney Carter comments: 'This allows for a different vocation for each human being. S/he is not condemned to try impossibly to be a carbon copy of the Jesus who lived in Palestine' (*Dance in the Dark*, p. 49).

If we look at it this way, obedience to God begins to look a little different from the words of that carol, and in terms of the first phase of the Christian life very different. It is not 'doing what you are told' by some external authority or conforming yourself to some standard way. It is obeying the direction of your inmost being, doing what in your heart of hearts you love to do. Looked at from this perspective, Psalm 119 with its emphasis on the statutes, commandments and precepts of the Lord, becomes a wonderfully accurate expression of Christian longing, of the desire to live and to give what you are: 'I open my mouth and draw in my breath, for I yearn for your commandments' (verse 131).

So if this is the way in which we are to follow Christ, then we need to get to know him for ourselves, in order to find encouragement in living our own lives. We need to find a way of letting him into our lives as an inner guide and encourager. You need to discover who he is to you and who you are to him; in other words to make some contact with him which is personal to you. The next exercise is a way of making a start on that process using a particular method of meditation.

(There is a tape which could help you with this, available from the address on p. 207.)

AN EXERCISE

1. Choose an event from one of the gospels. Choose one that you find attractive, one that draws you.
2. Make sure you will be undisturbed for at least half an hour. First, take a few minutes to prepare yourself by becoming present: use the method from Chapter 4 that you found easiest.
3. Read through your chosen passage once or twice to familiarise yourself with it.
4. Let the scene take shape in your mind's eye: picture it as vividly as you can. Don't worry about whether it is historically or geographically accurate: let your imagination create the scene for you. For example, if the scene is the Sea of Galilee, picture a lake: see it, smell the air, get into a boat. What is it like? Feel the motion of it, hear the sounds, and so on. When the scene seems real to you, don't just picture it from a distance, be there in it yourself. When you feel reasonably at home in it, then go on.
5. Let the event take place before your eyes, with you in it: be there as the event takes place. You may find that you picture yourself as one of the central characters, for example, Peter in the boat, or someone asking for healing, and so on; or you may be a bystander, a member of the crowd. If you find that your role changes in the course of your time of prayer, that is fine. Allow to happen what will. Often something unplanned happening is an indication that you are really involved. Hear the words that are spoken by the central characters, see people's actions

and reactions, and allow your own reactions to happen without questioning them: it is important that you are there as yourself; don't try to be something you are not, or play a part that does not feel as though it is you. Don't worry if your imagination does not follow the Bible exactly: for example, supposing you find yourself as the sick man unable to get up when Jesus calls you, tell him what you feel, be as open and straightforward as you can. Be aware of how he responds. Ask any questions you wish: make any comments that occur to you.

6. When the event is concluded, you have time to be with Jesus and he has unlimited time for you. Take this opportunity to talk to him about what has just happened and your feelings about it. Listen for what he has to say. You may find that you converse with Jesus quite naturally. If you find it difficult to begin with, practice will help. Some find it easier to do this part in writing: you write what you want to say; and then wait for the response that seems to come from Jesus and write that down; then write your reply, an honest expression of your reaction; and so on. It is a matter of saying what you really feel and opening yourself to hear what Jesus may be saying. It is more a matter of allowing it than forcing it. If you feel you haven't anything to say, simply take time to be with him.

7. Write down in your journal what actually happened in your time of meditation (not what ought to have happened!). Reflect on what connections there may be between what happened in your meditation time and your daily life. Did your choice of passage and what happened have anything to say to you about how you are with God and how God is with you at this point in your life?

The aim of all this is a *present* encounter with Jesus. The means to it is the use of a gospel event and your imagination. If you find it difficult to use your imagination in this way, practice will help. We all have the capacity to picture and to imagine, but most of us have not been taught to exercise this capacity and to develop it. We may even have been taught that the use of the imagination is misleading and dangerous! But it is a God-given capacity of great value and importance, and we shall have reason to cultivate it further in Chapter 13.

For the faint-hearted, however, here are one or two points to note. First, if the very idea of Jesus turns you off, you may have to lay some ghosts from your past in order to open yourself to discovering him as an inner guide. You do not *have* to be ruled by your past. Secondly you do not need to have been to Israel or to be knowledgeable in history or archaeology to picture the scene of your event. Allow your imagination to create the context for you, and if it turns out to be modern and western, so be it. Knowing more of the customs and circumstances of first-century Palestine will of course be a help and an aid, but relying too much on memory or on intellectual knowledge *can* be a hindrance to your imagination.

Sometimes people worry that this kind of meditation is only projection, and that it says more about us than it says about Jesus. That is true, as far as it goes, and is half the intention in any case. In this kind of meditation you are apt to stumble over your own attitudes and feelings about Jesus. A friend in a meditation on 'Behold, I stand at the door and knock' found herself in a bare room with Jesus outside knocking and herself holding the door handle tightly to prevent him coming in! But the other half of the intention is to discover how Jesus actually is. This is the point of using gospel passages and not just untrammelled imagination. I have suggested using gospel *events*, at least to start with, because it is easier. But often simply a saying or a sentence from the gospels will suffice; your imagination will do the rest. And if at any time Jesus seems to act out of character, tell him straight. Your honest and forthright reactions will be a help in penetrating any of your projections that may get in the way. And if at first you find it difficult to talk to Jesus, talk to one of the other people in your chosen scene.

Finally if this method is new to you, you might think it is new-fangled. But in fact it has been in use by Christians for many centuries. It was developed into a system of spiritual journeying by St Ignatius Loyola and is offered in a modernised form in many retreat centres today.

(Information about all sorts of retreats and retreat centres can be found in *Retreats*, obtainable from The National Retreat Association, The Central Hall, 256 Bermondsey Street, London SE1 3UJ.)

AN UNEXPECTED COMPANION

That same day two of them were on their way to a village called Emmaus, which lay about seven miles from Jerusalem, and they were talking together about all these happenings. As they talked and discussed it with one another, Jesus himself came up and walked along with them; but something held their eyes from seeing who it was. He asked them, 'What is it you are debating as you walk?' They halted, their faces full of gloom, and one, called Cleopas, answered, 'Are you the only person staying in Jerusalem not to know what has happened there in the last few days?' 'What do you mean?' he said. 'All this about Jesus of Nazareth,' they replied, 'a prophet powerful in speech and action before God and the whole people; how our chief priests and rulers handed him over to be sentenced to death, and crucified him. But we had been hoping that he was the man to liberate Israel. What is more, this is the third day since it happened, and now some women of our company have astounded us: they went early to the tomb, but failed to find his body, and returned with a story that they had seen a vision of angels who told them he was alive. So some of our people went to the tomb and found things just as the women had said; but him they did not see.'

'How dull you are!' he answered. 'How slow to believe all that the prophets said! Was the Messiah not bound to suffer thus before entering upon his glory?' Then he began with Moses and all the prophets, and explained to them the passages which referred to himself in every part of the scriptures.

By this time they had reached the village to which they were going, and he made as if to continue his journey, but they pressed him: 'Stay with us, for evening draws on, and the day is almost over.' So he went in to stay with them. And when he had sat down with them at table, he took bread and said the blessing; he broke the bread, and offered it to them. Then their eyes were opened, and they recognised him; and he vanished from their sight. They said to one another, 'Did we not feel our hearts on fire as he talked with us on the road and explained the scriptures to us?' (Luke 24:13–32)

7

Listen to Your Story

Joe used to sell hot crispy potatoes from a barrow which he parked outside the old Theatre Royal in Sunderland. He was widely known in the town and plied his trade until some time in the 1950s. In 1976, while I was vicar of a Sunderland parish we had a parish weekend at Scargill House in the Yorkshire Dales, which we entitled 'My story, your story, our story'. On the first evening one of our congregation showed some slides of life in Sunderland. The first one was of Tatie Joe. There was a delighted cry of recognition from the eighty or so people round the room. I sensed that it was all the more heartfelt because we were in a foreign land, Yorkshire! It expressed the sense of shared story, one of the strongest links that bind people together.

An important part of our identity is communal. This can be a great force for good, a strong shared identity in which individuals can be nurtured in spirit and from which they can grow. Laurens van der Post writes: 'These people [the Kalahari bushmen] knew what we do not: that without a story you have not got a nation, or a culture, or a civilisation. Without a story of your own to live, you haven't got a life of your own.' But perhaps because it is so necessary, it can also be a prison, a kind of invisible wall for the mind and spirit, which prevents us seeing and stunts our growth and can even take us for a ride.

An example of this was provided by the Falklands conflict of 1982. Whatever you think now about the rights and wrongs of going to war on that issue, there is no doubt that at the time the reason why there was such widespread uncritical acceptance that it was right was because it tuned in to our British national 'story' or myth. Our national myth is of course that we are an island people, fiercely independent, beholden to no one, who 'never, never, never shall be slaves'. To object to our country going to war on behalf of those beleaguered fellow-islanders in the South Atlantic was regarded as treasonable. It was extremely difficult to argue that you could be patriotic while not agreeing with the war. It was beyond argument: at that time we British were 'possessed' by our national myth.

Is 'possession' too strong a word? Perhaps it is easier to see in other nations. It was certainly true of Germany in the 1930s when the nation was possessed by the superman myth. It is easy for us to look back and wonder how they could be so deluded. But being 'possessed' by a story, being lived by it, is an exhilarating experience. It needs a good deal of self-awareness to take a more conscious responsibility for your life and your actions. It needs a willingness to 'die' to that sense of exhilaration, a willingness to swim against the tide of popular sentiment. In particular it means taking more conscious responsibility for the darker side of our nature and its effects on others. As the followers of C. G. Jung are fond of reminding us, the brighter the vision the darker the shadow it is liable to cast in its outworking.

So there is a danger, as well as great value, in a sense of shared story in our life. For humanity's health we need a story, a dream, a hope which transcends social and national boundaries; we need a world hope that can take us beyond the jingoism of class or nation. And we need one that can speak both to individuals and to society. I believe we have these qualities in the Exodus saga, that archetypal journey out of slavery towards a new country, with all the hopes and the longings, and all the backsliding and buckpassing that went on on the way.

The best stories speak to the widest circle of people. Such

are fairy stories, and on a larger scale myths. They distil
the common universal elements of human experience.
Some are so completely 'distilled' that they are abstractions
of human experience, so much so that they do not tell you
how the hero felt as he walked into the giant's cave, they
simply tell you baldly that he went in.

The 'story of Jesus' needs to be, and in the gospels is,
told in this universal way; not as the story of one person,
but as the story of The Person. His 'story' distils the essential features of the Christian life, as we saw in the last
chapter. However, many people view him as an impossibly
exalted hero and this can be a great barrier. Others over-
identify with him in a 'whiter than white' kind of way,
which is the equal and opposite danger. The fact is that
reading the life of Christ without its Old Testament background can damage your spiritual health. It needs as a
background, in a somewhat less elevated form, the saga of
the Exodus and the journey to the new land. In some ways
that can provide us with a more earthy link between us
and the Jesus story.

It can be quite an interesting exercise to read through
that saga at one sitting. You could include Exodus,
Numbers from Chapter 9 on, the end of Deuteronomy and
the first few chapters of Joshua. Skip the lists of rules,
leave out the instructions about offerings, the directions
for building the Ark of the Covenant, and so on. Get a
quick overall impression. If you like, abbreviate it still
further and simply read Exodus 1–20 and Numbers 11–14.
If you are unfamiliar with these books of the Bible, they
may seem full of violence and injustice. It is important to
see beyond the literal meaning of this saga. It is not just
about the Jews or about the Church. It is about the promise
of God's kingdom for all, where all can flourish. It is about
the hope for that state of affairs where oppression, injustice,
prejudice and blindness are no more, a state of both social
wholeness and individual fulfilment.

There is within everyone a longing for a new land. It
may get trivialised into the new car or the summer holiday,
the new house, the new job or the latest gadget. But it

seems that part of being human is to have this longing which always draws our hearts to what we hope will be a better future. It is to this longing that the Exodus saga speaks. As you read it notice the people in it with whom you identify. Be aware of your feelings about what they do and what happens to them. Does it illuminate aspects of your own life and experience? Do you for example sometimes feel like an Israelite brickmaker, weighed down by unremitting and unrewarding toil, waiting for someone to set you free? Have you sometimes felt as Moses did? You may well have done if at some time in your life you have taken a creative initiative, perhaps with a sense of being prompted by God, that meant swimming against the stream of others' expectations. You may be familiar with the feelings of inadequacy and unworthiness. You will almost certainly have had the experience of being blamed and battered when things go wrong. You may be familiar also with the strange sense that in spite of all the difficulties and frustrations the wind is mysteriously behind you. In the last few years I have felt some sympathy with Caleb. He was one of the small party that was sent ahead to explore the new land. They returned with some of its rich produce, but some of the exploring party exaggerated the problems they would encounter. Caleb stood out for going ahead. He did not deny the problems, but reminded them that it was at God's invitation that they had set out. God would be with them.

The Exodus saga then, is the story of a journey from oppression and unremitting toil to a new land. It is both a corporate hope for humanity and an exemplar of an individual journey. We are each personally called to a 'new land'. You are called to unearth your treasure, to live your giftedness, to have a whale of a time doing what you are for. That is for many people a new and unexplored land. Drawing on the imagery of another biblical journey, Martin Buber writes:

God said to Abraham: 'Get thee out of thy country, and from thy kindred, and from thy father's house, unto the land that I will show thee.' God says to man: 'First, get you out of your country, that means the dimness you have inflicted on yourself. Then out of your birthplace, that means out of the dimness your mother inflicted on you. After that, out of the house of your father, that means out of the dimness your father inflicted on you. Only then will you be able to go to the land that I will show you.' (*Ten Rungs*, Schocken Books, 1947, p. 70)

We are called out of our past to a new country, to our tiny part in the journey to that corporate new land which is the kingdom of God. And though its complete fulfilment awaits us hereafter, we are to begin to live the kingdom life in this world. This means crawling out from under the limited expectations and cramping assumptions of our past. It means coming to terms with what our past has made us. It means accepting and integrating the wounds and scars sustained in our younger days. It means being animated and energised by some purpose we seek to realise in the future. It means leaving the familiar, and setting out on an unknown way.

This is not a journey we decide to take on our own initiative; we take it at God's invitation. God calls each of us from the womb, from our very conception. God calls us by our unique name, which only s/he knows. As Metropolitan Anthony so eloquently puts it, that

> is a name, a word, which is exactly identified with us, which coincides with us, which *is* us. You may almost say it is a word which God pronounced when he willed us into existence and which is us, as we are it. This name defines our absolute and unrepeatable uniqueness as far as God is concerned. (*School for Prayer*, DLT, 1970 and 1999, p. 66)

So it is God who calls us into being, like the creation of man in Genesis 2:7: 'The Lord God formed a man from the dust of the ground'; and the word 'formed' is the word used of working clay. Irenaeus uses the same metaphor in a lovely instruction: 'Offer your heart to God in a soft and tractable state that you may receive the impress of his fingers, lest being hardened you should escape his workmanship and your life.' God does not just call us into existence, s/he calls us into being what we can be; and that being includes doing. What we are is to issue in what we do. What we do is to proceed from what we are.

So our life is a journey of becoming, and also a journey into action. And there needs to be an integral link between our being and our doing. The task to which God calls us arises out of what we are in our deepest selves; s/he calls out from us the energy and vitality that flows from our inmost centre. This whole process is much easier to describe than it is to live. But as we grow older we do sometimes become aware of a mysterious thread that runs through the years of our life. I use the word thread as a metaphor for personal meaning, that central sense of story or purposiveness in our being and doing that sometimes becomes clear to us. The image of the thread may make it sound as though it is predetermined, laid down in advance like a railway track. But a thread is much flimsier and infinitely more flexible than that. It is almost as though, like a silkworm, we spin the thread as we go; the story of your life is not written in advance, you write it in the living of each day. And yet your living of it day by day does not automatically give expression to what you might call the underlying story of your life. It may diverge very considerably from it. At those times you are far from being on your thread. And this underlying story is not some idealised purified version, with the naughty bits and the mistakes and your disabilities removed. On the contrary it is that mysterious process of moving towards wholeness that integrates what you are towards what you could become and what you could give. 'God made man', writes Elie Wiesel, 'because he loves stories.'

So the exercise at the end of this chapter offers a way of looking at your life up to now, of becoming more aware of your own story, of how God has brought you to this point, of how you have sought or avoided or misperceived

. . . far from being on your thread

God's leading. It offers you an opportunity to become more aware of your searching for God, and in particular through the words of the Psalms to begin to hear your own voice calling out to God. In short it is one way of discovering who God is with you and who you are with God, because it is in that relationship that God's call to you to action is heard. As Sam Keen says, 'If I am to discover the holy, it must be in my biography and not in the history of Israel' (*To a Dancing God*, p. 99).

You may feel that this is to take a very individualistic view of our life. The short answer is that if you are to take your part in a generous and full-blooded way in the corporate journey to the new country, it will require also a thorough-going engagement in the individual journey. No one else can make your personal part of that journey for you. It is sometimes a temptation to expect that 'the group', whatever form that may take, will carry you along. When that happens you will find yourself an Israelite abdicating your part in the corporate process and grumbling at the mess the leaders are making of it. The fact is that there are times when each of us is to be a Moses. Each of us is to be willing to stick our neck out, to take initiatives, to stand alone when it is required, in however small ways; for of such is the kingdom of God. The corporate humanity-wide wholeness that we are promised and hope for is to be a society of differentiated persons. Genuine community happens when everyone takes the risk and the responsibility of exercising their gift, but in such a way as to enable others to do the same. Too often our seeking for community is an avoidance of that hard but fulfilling road.

AN EXERCISE

Take a large sheet of paper, at least the size of two 29 × 21 cm sheets placed end to end. Draw a straight line across the middle along the longest axis. Write along it the main events of your life in chronological order. You will probably find it a help to list them before you start writing along the line. Put into the list any events that seem significant to you.

Now using the lower half of the paper, and in different colours, write single words or phrases that describe your feelings about the various events in your life, putting the high

INTERESTED
(Sunday
school)

LIVELY
(Young people's
group)

GOD FELT
CLOSE

MORE ADULT
INTEREST
(Took instruction for
church membership)

MADE
REDUNDANT

PROMOTION
AT WORK

NUMBNESS
TURNING
TO ANGER

MARRIAGE

FLATTERED

ON TOP OF
THE WORLD

LET DOWN
(Gave up church going)

BORED
(Taken to church)

MOTHER
DIED

FIRST JOB

DESOLATE

MOVED
HOUSE

PROUD

FRIENDSHIP
WITH TOM

FRIENDLESS
AND ALIEN

STARTED
SCHOOL

COMPANIONABLE

HOLIDAYS BY
THE SEASIDE

PUSHED
OUT

FUN WITH
FAMILY

Sample Lifeline

spots higher and the low spots lower as your feelings about them seem to require. When you have finished writing these in, join them up with a line as in the diagram.

Then using the top half of the paper jot down in a similar way your feelings about God at different points. Add in also any special events that did not find a place on the centre line. Join these up with a line.

Finally, look for verses or half verses from the Psalms that most nearly express your feelings towards God at the different points in your life. Write them in wherever appropriate in either the top or bottom half of the paper. If you are unfamiliar with the Psalms, the following express varied moods: 27, 38, 88, 103, 121, 126 and 139; you could start by looking through these. In any case you will probably need to do this part of the exercise a bit at a time over a period of days. When you have done it you could write out the verses you have chosen in your journal in the chronological order in which they appear on your lifeline. That is then *your* Psalm, the expression of your feelings towards God in your history, just as for the original writers the Psalms expressed their history.

You may find that this exercise brings back painful memories as well as pleasant and happy ones. If you feel they are too much to cope with, perhaps you should look for a counsellor or good listener who will help you express your feelings and come to better terms with your past. Sometimes people think they have 'put it behind them' when they have succeeded in suppressing their feelings about a painful event. Then something happens which raises them all over again, and they feel impatient with themselves. Try to be a little more tolerant and patient with yourself. This is all part of the lifelong journey towards wholeness. Julian of Norwich has some encouraging words: 'Though the soul's wounds heal, the scars remain. God sees them not as blemishes but as honours' (*Revelations of Divine Love*, ch. 39). In time they may even turn out to be gifts.

If you have difficulty finding a counsellor, the British Association for Counselling publishes a list, obtainable from the Association at 37A Sheep Street, Rugby CV21 3BX.

THE SCULPTOR

A child was taken to see a sculptor at work. He watched him wielding the hammer and chisel and the chips of stone flying this way and that. But he could see no recognisable shape, because work on this particular block of stone had only just begun.

A few weeks later he was taken to the workshop again. The artist showed him the completed sculpture. The child stared in amazement: 'How did you know there was a lion in there?'

8

'Disabilities' Might Become Gifts

In eighteenth-century France to be blind was regarded as a punishment from God. Blind people were condemned at best to be beggars, at worst derided figures of entertainment, in a circus as gladiators, or in an 'orchestra' dressed as idiots in dunce's caps scraping away tunelessly on instruments for the amusement of fair-goers. It was a scene such as that at the Foire St Ovide that deeply shocked a young man named Valentin Haüy on an autumn day in 1771. Some weeks later on his way out of church on Sunday, Haüy passed a blind boy begging by the roadside, and put some coins in his outstretched hands. He noticed how the boy carefully felt the coins to check their value, and realised that for him his fingers were his eyes. It was the beginning of a friendship between him and the boy, François Lesueur, whom he laboriously taught to read by means of raised letters, first carved on wood blocks, and later embossed on the pages of books. Eventually he opened the first school in the world for blind children.

This was all to be swept away by the French Revolution. But later, when Louis Braille, aged 10, first went to school at the re-founded Institut Royale des Jeunes Aveugles in Paris, that was the system that was in use. Braille was the youngest child of a saddler, and as a toddler was often looked after by his father in his workshop. One day in the summer of 1812 there was an accident – no one knows exactly how, but little Louis cut into the eyeball of his right eye with a sharp tool of some kind. Within a few months both his eyes were affected by the injury and he became totally blind.

Louis Braille was by all accounts a very intelligent child and found the Haüy method of reading frustratingly slow. When a new system of teaching the blind to read was offered for trial at the Institut, he was one of the young people invited to try it out. It had been invented as 'night writing' by one Captain Charles Barbier for use in the army so that soldiers could read instructions at night without giving away their position by lighting a lamp. It had been turned down by the military authorities as not worth bothering with. But Barbier was very proud of his invention and decided it would be a help in teaching the blind to read.

The children who tried it quickly realised its limitations. It was a kind of embossed shorthand, quicker to read if you knew the words already, but no help at all in basic education. But Barbier still persisted in promoting his invention, reckoning he knew more than a few blind schoolchildren. The director of the Institut perceptively commented that Barbier's 'need for self-gratification had become more important than trying to understand the true and real needs of the blind'. However, the method had sown the seeds of an idea in the mind of the 15-year-old Louis, who for months was to spend every spare moment trying to work out a way of reading for the blind that took account of the fact that it is not the eyes which read words, as sighted people suppose, but the brain.

It is instructive to compare the approach of those three men, Haüy, Barbier and Braille. Haüy was genuinely concerned to do something to help blind children. But though he took endless trouble and gave his life to this work, he had no experience of blindness himself. Barbier is a classic example of a do-gooder whose ego was massively in the way, too proud to listen, and hopelessly over-identified with his 'baby'. It took Braille, blind himself from the age of three, to refine a system that would actually be a help to blind children learning to read.

Often, it seems, a personal characteristic that the owner has thought of as a handicap or problem, or an event that has been regarded as a misfortune or even a disaster, has turned out to be an important factor in what that person has done with their life. Another famous instance of this is to be seen in the life of Alexander Graham Bell. Throughout his life he was a very private and solitary person. His son-in-law said of him after his death, 'Mr Bell led a peculiarly isolated life; I have never known anyone who spent so much of his time alone'. He used to do much of his work as an inventor at night. In a letter to his wife in 1890 he wrote, 'I feel more and more as I grow older the tendency to retire into myself and be alone with my thoughts. I can see the same tendency in my father and uncle. . . . My children have it too. . . . You alone are free from it – and you my dear constitute the chief link between myself and the world outside.' This is remarkable, since Bell's wife was totally deaf as a result of scarlet fever contracted at the age of five, although she was a very accomplished lip reader. His mother, too, had been deaf; and both his father and grandfather were teachers of elocution. Add to that his great musical ability – at one point he considered a career as a pianist – and his interest in sound and speech and communication is not surprising. At the age of 21 he began what proved to be a lifelong concern, the teaching of deaf children to speak. His best-known protégée and friend was Helen Keller, who had been deaf and blind since she was 19 months old. It is interesting to reflect that this was the man who gave the world the telephone, one of the most important aids to direct communication between people that has so far been invented.

Louis Braille and Alexander Bell are very striking examples of people for whom a problem or handicap or disability became a kind of gift; in the sense that because of it, either directly or indirectly, they came to offer something quite special to the world. But this factor commonly operates among 'ordinary' people. I have been aware of it in my own life. I have already mentioned in earlier chapters the 'dutiful' Christianity in which I was brought up. It was really only out of a sense of duty that I offered myself for ordination. In terms of my personal inclination I could not think of anything I wanted to do less, and I devoutly hoped the selectors would turn me down. For me personally, with that sort of background, ordination felt like a knuckling under to a kind of death-in-life, an entry into a sort of imprisonment. That may sound a rather extreme way to put it. But, looking back, that was how I felt about it at the time I was ordained in 1960. As the years went by, and as I gradually crawled out from under those attitudes, I was able to do some creative work and to enjoy a lot of what I did as a parish priest. But there was always, if I was honest with myself, an element of that underlying feeling lurking beneath the surface. It was only very slowly and painfully that I came to understand that the gospel is *good* news, and that *premature* self-abnegation and 'shouldering the cross' is actually an avoidance of life – and of course a misunderstanding of the true meaning of the cross.

So in my case it was a strong overdose in my youth of 'dutiful Christianity' that was my particular burden – a kind of handicap, I suppose. But that period of 'imprisonment', for more than 20 years, forced me to think long and hard and deep about vocation and the calling of God, to wrestle with questions like: What is it to be truly called by God? What sort of people does God call? To what sort of things? Is it always to something painful or unwelcome?

Do I regret this episode in my life? Whatever I felt at the time, how could I regret it now? It has been the means by which I have come to a fuller life than I could possibly have dreamed of. It has brought me to the work which I now love to do, the task of re-defining the idea of vocation, and, through writing, running workshops and talking to individuals, encouraging people to find fulfilment and fruitfulness by responding to God's invitation to them. I do not think I personally could have come to this any other way. It was a journey that had to be taken, a journey of discovery that the gospel is indeed *good* news.

Some may think that life should not be like this, that my offering myself for ordination in that frame of mind was the result of neurosis, not the calling of God at all. I shall have a bit more to say about that in Chapter 16. For now, I would say that anyone who sees it like that has been seduced by the Greek/Renaissance view of the perfectibility of humankind; Michelangelo's David, the human being as Greek god, physically perfect, without visible blemish. That notion is prevalent in this modern age in the various therapies and nostrums that promise to remove all the blemishes from your skin, all the flaws from your appearance and all the ailments from your body. In Christian circles it makes its appearance as the search for total healing, where healing means getting rid of all the wounds and disabilities and blemishes, as though they were detachable, removable without leaving a trace. That is in origin not a Christian notion, and it betokens a very shallow idea of what constitutes health. A doctor friend told me that some years ago he resigned from general practice because he felt more and more strongly that cure gets in the way of genuine healing. A simple example of this is the common or garden heart attack. Doctors set out to relieve the heart condition without doing anything about the lifestyle that causes it.

Truer to the Christian idea of what it is to be a mature and healthy person is the wounded healer. It may be that some wounds or disabilities can indeed be cured, in the sense of being removed without trace. I am all for that where it is possible. But I think for many of us 'healing' is more like coming to some sort of terms with our traumas and handicaps, even 'befriending' them, rather than simply being able to be rid of them. In the process many of us begin to discern that they can be a kind of gift, an inalienable aspect of our very selves, through which we are invited by God to be gift to others. They are also a healthy reminder that becoming a perfect specimen of humanity is not the overriding purpose of life.

Elizabeth O'Connor writes, 'The larger sorrows do not . . . readily go away, and may be intricately related to the work we are to do'. What may seem to you like a problem, or disability, or disaster is often an important factor in the discernment of what God is calling you to do. It is not always a factor however. And when it is, it will not be the only one. Sometimes you may not realise how important a factor it was for you until you look back over your life. But I think all of us have something like this that dogs us, hampers us, keeps us in chains, prevents us taking wings; something we have to engage with, wrestle with, fight with even, until we come to some sort of terms with it and can allow it to give us its blessing. And because of it we may perhaps eventually, at God's invitation, become a blessing to others.

In case what I have said so far seems 'writ large', perhaps off-puttingly so, let me end this section with a less conspicuous example of the kind of thing I mean. When I was a teenager (although we were not called that in those days) I was painfully, even pathologically, shy. When I run workshops now people tell me that though my leadership is firm, it is gentle. Perhaps it is because of my extreme sensitivity as a youngster that I now have some awareness of other people's feelings when they feel vulnerable.

AN EXERCISE

Consider your personal characteristics, circumstances, the things that have happened to you: is there anything you think of as a flaw, defect or disability? Any problem, difficulty or burden? Any wound, trauma, or disaster?

Take some time to reflect on this question – have any of these at some time or in some situations turned out to be a kind of gift? In what way?

A PARABLE

Each day the king sat in state hearing petitions and dispensing justice. Each day a holy man, dressed in the robe of an ascetic beggar, approached the king and without a word offered him a piece of very ripe fruit. Each day the king accepted the 'present' from the beggar, handed it to his treasurer who stood behind the throne, and thought no more about it. Each day the beggar, again without a word, withdrew and disappeared into the crowd.

Year after year this same little ritual occurred every day the king sat in office. One day, about ten years after the holy man first appeared, something different happened. A tame monkey, having escaped from the women's apartments in the inner palace, came bounding into the hall and leapt up onto the arm of the king's throne. The beggar had just presented the king with his usual gift of fruit; but this time instead of passing it to his treasurer the king gave it to the monkey. When the animal bit into it a precious jewel dropped out and fell on the floor.

The king was amazed and quickly turned to his treasurer, 'What has become of all the others?' The treasurer had no answer. Every time he had simply thrown the unimpressive 'gifts' through a small upper window in the treasure house, not even bothering to unlock the door. So he hurriedly excused himself and ran to the vault. He opened the door and quickly made for the area beneath the little window. There on the floor lay a mass of rotten fruit in various stages of decay. But amid all the rubbish of so many years could be seen dozens and dozens of precious jewels.

9

Know Yourself to be Loved by God

'The best prayer is to rest in the goodness of God, knowing that that goodness can reach right down to our lowest depths of need.' If those words of Julian of Norwich speak to you, there is no need for you to read any further in this chapter. Instead of reading on, take time to 'be' in God's presence and let God's love percolate through to the deepest and darkest recesses of your nature. Know yourself to be loved through and through just as you are, without any strings or conditions attached.

For many of us, however, it is not as easy as that. There are many things that prevent us being able to receive the love of God. Sometimes in a guided meditation at a retreat or a workshop I use the words spoken from heaven to Jesus at his baptism in St Mark's Gospel, Chapter 1, and ask the retreatants to hear those words spoken to each of them personally: 'You are my daughter, my beloved, I delight in you.' 'You are my son, my beloved, I delight in you.' At the end of one such retreat someone commented: 'Those words quite shattered my composure; I went back to my room and had a good weep.' On another occasion, at a series of evening sessions on prayer, the participants were asked to use those words as the theme for their own praying between sessions. The following week one person was brave enough to say that she had not been able to use those words at all: she simply could not imagine that God could possibly love her. At a parish weekend one person reported that she had been unable to stomach the words 'I delight in you'. For her they conjured up the image of a cat playing with a mouse. It reminded me of those terrible words at the end of Thomas Hardy's *Tess of the d'Urbervilles*: 'The president of the immortals had finished his sport with Tess.'

Those different reactions illustrate how varied can be the barriers to receiving the love of God. For one it is little more than the barrier of convention: that since it is more blessed to give than to receive, somehow it is not done to be on the receiving end of things. For another what stands in the way is the deep conviction that she is unlovable. For another it is the unconscious 'knowledge' that God is a sadist.

In Chapter 4 when I was talking about being present I alluded in passing to the similarity between our relationship with God and our relationship with other people, at least if you look at it from the human standpoint. There is a similar parallelism in the matter of being loved. I suppose you could say that in this regard there are roughly three sorts of people. First there are the friendly and trusting people who basically do not find relationships a problem. Deep down they know they are loved. Their prayer life will have its ups and downs but they will not be afflicted by doubts about God's goodness or by long periods when God seems to have taken himself off. If you are one of these fortunate people, the present chapter will be unnecessary for you personally, though it may help you to understand others.

Secondly there are people who are friendly and outgoing and relate easily on the surface but whose underlying motivation for this is fear of loneliness or desertion. They inwardly feel very unlovable and therefore feel the need to try to make people love them, by winning ways, manipulation, clinging, acting a part, and so on. For these folk, control is the key issue. But of course to make genuine relationships you need to let go of your desire to manipulate other people to love you, and that means facing the inner fear of desertion. If that is to some extent true of your human relationships it will probably surface sooner or later in your relationship with God. Often a person of this kind, as they come to know God, will have quite a 'honeymoon' period that may last a year or two. But after a while the good feelings may become less frequent and may eventually dry up altogether. You then face what may be long periods of the apparent absence of God. S/he seems to leave you in darkness with no reassuring awareness of presence; and if there are fleeting times when s/he seems to return, they are unexpected and unpredictable, beyond your control. Many writers on prayer describe this condition. A recent one who does so in a very down to earth way is Thomas H. Green. He says, and it makes sense to me, that for this type of person the function of the darkness is to purge the desire to control God's comings and goings.

Thomas Green tends to give the impression, as do many other writers, that what he says will apply to most people if they progress far enough. But his comparison with human relationships makes me think that what he describes is *not* in fact everyone's road, however far on they are. He writes:

> The emotions, those feelings which have a strong element of sense and imagination in them, are a good and necessary part of the whole human being. But they are essentially self-centred . . . It is this kind of 'love' which makes for intense courtships and short marriages, since even in marriage the well of emotion will surely run dry as the honeymoon is followed by the ordinary routine days. (*When The Well Runs Dry,* Ave Maria Press, 1980, pp. 23–4)

It is particularly that last sentence that gives me pause. What he describes is certainly the experience of some. It is equally certainly not the experience of others, for whom love in marriage begins gradually and not in a great burst of emotion, and slowly deepens and ripens as the years pass.

In short I believe that in terms of these rough and ready

groupings there is a third type of person. These are the frozen, shy or reticent people who do not express their feelings easily. They feel inwardly unlovable as well, but with an intensity that causes them to avoid relationships. They are not afraid of God or others deserting them. They are afraid of God approaching them. For these folk, being loved is a frightening prospect. To allow God to approach is to open themselves to fears that they feel instinctively will annihilate them. For them the darkness is not empty; as they enter it they may find it is peopled by malevolent monsters. This has been my own experience: my journey towards God has meant encountering some of these before ever I experienced any emotional closeness to God. Small wonder that some are in their hearts agnostics or sceptics. Belief in God, especially a loving God, is too alarming to contemplate.

Now of course we human beings do not fall neatly into categories, and it certainly does not help to try and pigeon-hole either ourselves or others. But it can be just as unhelpful if a general statement about people's experience of God is made as though it applied to everyone. I certainly find it useful to make this rough and ready threefold distinction that I have tried to describe.

To put it briefly, for some a honeymoon time is natural and to be expected; but it need not dismay you if the good feelings do not last: God is no less with you, even if you do not feel anything. For others it may be many years before you even *begin* to be aware of good feelings about God. There is no need to feel left out because a honeymoon never seems to come: it is simply that that is not your way; but it does not mean that God does not exist or does not care. In fact for the more deeply wounded folk God's tender, unintrusive care is all the greater.

For yet others the problems I have described will feel totally foreign; their feelings about God are simply not problematical.

So wherever you stand in this matter be patient with yourself, and also with others whose experiences and attitudes are different from yours. Take to heart the words of Meister Eckhart: 'How can anyone be compassionate towards her neighbour who is not compassionate towards herself? This is why Jesus says: be compassionate! He wants our compassion to begin at home. He wants us to be compassionate towards our own body and soul' (Matthew Fox, *Meditations with Meister Eckhart*, p. 105). One might add that for some this is the first step towards allowing themselves to be loved by God. Others are fortunate enough to learn it through experiences of love and acceptance from another human being.

The importance of self-acceptance was much underlined by Jung, both for the psychotherapist and for the religious person: for the former because without it she can be of no real help to another; for the latter because 'he knows that God has brought all sorts of strange and inconceivable things to pass, and seeks in the most curious ways to enter a man's heart. He therefore senses in everything the unseen presence of the divine will.' Jung goes on, in a justly famous passage, to say how very difficult self-acceptance is:

The acceptance of oneself is the essence of the moral problem and the epitome of a whole outlook upon life. That I feed the hungry, that I forgive an insult, that I love my enemy in the name of Christ – all these are undoubtedly great virtues. What I do unto the least of my brethren, that I do unto Christ. But what if I should discover that the least among them all, the poorest of all the beggars, the most impudent of all the offenders, the very enemy himself – that these are within me and that I myself stand in need of the alms of my own kindness – that I myself am the enemy who must be loved – what then? As a rule, the Christian's attitude is then reversed; there is no longer any question of love or long-suffering; we say to the brother within us 'Raca' (i.e. fool, idiot) and condemn and rage against ourselves. We hide it from the world; we refuse to admit ever having met this least among the lowly in ourselves. Had it been God himself who drew near to us in this despicable form, we should have denied him a thousand times before a single cock had crowed. (*Modern Man in Search of a Soul*, Routledge, 1933, pp. 271–2)

Strong words, you may think; surely no one is that much at odds with themselves. Well, many are, and many others come to an awareness of this as they grow older.

Jesus' comparison of the kingdom with a banquet to which *all* are invited is a help here. In the latter part of this chapter I want to spend a little time unpacking this comparison because I believe it is an image of wholeness, individual wholeness within ourselves, and corporate wholeness as a human race, both of which are to be the outcome of allowing ourselves to be loved by God.

Let me start with the corporate aspect. The most obvious meaning of the banquet imagery is the outer, public one. For example Jesus says: 'When you give a feast, invite the poor, the maimed, the lame and the blind, and you will be blessed.' (Luke 14:1–14) He likens the kingdom of God to a banquet or party to which there is a special invitation to the poor, the disabled and the outcasts. Taken in its outer meaning it invites the conclusion that if society in this world is to reflect our hope and our longing for the kingdom of God, then we must in our social organisation be biased to the poor. There must be in the way our institutions function and our laws are framed a special concern for the disabled, the oppressed and the impoverished.

There has been some public debate in recent years in this country about the welfare state, about who should contribute to the common purse and how much, and about who are and who should be the beneficiaries. For example the Social Security reviews of the mid-eighties were a reminder of how visionary were the aims of the Beveridge proposals. Even in the modified form in which they were adopted in 1948 the intention was that social benefits were every citizen's right, not just 'charity' to bail you out if you got into difficulties. That is an appropriate way for society to be biased to the poor. Any other way singles out

the poor and makes them different. Even now, when benefits are every citizen's right, many older people do not
claim them because they think of them as 'charity'. They
still have associations in their minds with the Poor Law
approach: they feel a sense of shame about claiming as
though it were an admission of failure as a citizen. This is
an outer, public issue about what sort of society we want,
about how the poorer members of it feel, about whether
we organise it in such a way that they are made to feel
that they are not really members of it at all, that they are
only here on sufferance. Such questions are about much
more than the social welfare system: they are about how
our society can be ordered as far as possible so that
everyone can feel a valued part of it. And the question the
kingdom puts to our society is: Does *everyone* have a place
at the table?

This is to look at the image of the kingdom in terms of
its implications for the outer, public world. But, as John
Sanford in *The Kingdom Within*, and others who have built
on the work of Jung have taught us, many of Jesus' sayings
have at the same time implications for our inner lives, and
this one is no exception. The kingdom of God may be
likened to an inner banquet to which all the many aspects
of your nature are invited. And so if you are a seeker after
that kingdom there needs to be a special invitation to the
outcasts, the crippled, the impoverished and the unloved
among your inner population.

The phrase 'inner population' may sound a bit over the
top, as though I were speaking of multiple personalities,
of some rare case of extreme schizophrenia. Not a bit of it!
I use the phrase to point to ordinary everyday experience
of your inner life. Take an example: when your alarm goes
off in the morning you may turn over and think how much
you would like to stay in bed for another half an hour. But
after a minute or two you remember that today you are to
meet someone to discuss a project close to your heart. It is
as though part of you is weary and would love to have a
lie-in; another part of you is full of energy and wanting to
get on with your favourite project. I am inviting you

to think of those parts of you as selves, to personify those feelings, so that you can begin more consciously to befriend them and hear what they have to say to you, even if they seem to contradict one another. Perhaps this will begin to explain what I mean by your inner population.

Another example may help to clarify it a bit further. A few years ago a woman who was very clever came to talk to me. As a Christian she was worried by her scornful feelings towards people less able than herself. It gradually became clear to her that there was a part of *her* who was not clever but gauche and wanting to be loved. But she regarded this aspect of herself as weak and ruthlessly suppressed it. She looked upon this self as an idiot, a cretin. The question that faced her was, could she allow this idiot a place at her inner table? As she gradually found the courage to do so she found that this self had an important contribution to make to her inner 'body politic', that it was not as valueless as she had supposed.

For most of us there are 'selves' within us who are oppressed in one way or another, whom we too easily think of as weak or damaged or beyond the pale. Oppression is not only an outer, public issue! And of course there are inner selves who are oppressors, as we began to notice in Chapter 3; and these inner 'Pharaohs' are responsible for squashing a great deal of life and joy and creativity within us.

Because of this oppressive behaviour within, we are to go out into the streets and lanes of our inner life and search for the neglected, the incompetent, the young, the lame and the unloved. Each of them is to have a special invitation to the party. And among all these inner outcasts, we all have within us 'one of the least of these' – a part of ourselves whom we especially despise and want to disown, to get rid of, sometimes even 'to be healed of'.

I will come back to this last point in a moment, because this particularly brings us back to our theme. But first perhaps I should explain why I have brought in the outer, public dimension in this chapter, where on the face of it it might seem out of place. I have done so for two reasons.

First, because our attitude to our inner 'poor' very much affects our attitudes to the 'poor' in the outer world and vice versa. Suppression of or lack of awareness of the weak within makes us impatient of the weak in society and may make us blind to their problems or even to their existence. And this is after all a book about *linking* being and doing, about *connections* between prayer and action. Secondly, because for many of us that 'self' who could be a gift to the life of the outer world lies unnoticed in an inner junk room, or is known dimly but feared and shut out as a potential disturber of our peace. In other words in among the riff-raff lies the potential treasure. If we are to unearth our treasure it means moving in the direction of the kingdom in our inner life, so that in our inner world everyone may be valued and have a place at the table, especially the oppressed and those without a voice.

I said 'where everyone may be valued and have a place'. Does that include our inner critics, parrots and such? The short answer is, not unless they are willing to forswear their oppressive behaviour. An example might help to make this clear. A friend we will call John was aware of a part of him who used to say: 'John, you are completely worthless, your life isn't worth living.' He came to call this part of him the withering voice, because he felt it withered the life in him. When John and his wife had their first child the baby's yelling made him aware for the first time of an angry shouting self within him. He felt that this part of him was very much pro-life, but had been suppressed: he had always been told as a child that he should not cry or raise his voice. Clearly the angry little one had a right to have a place at his inner table and needed listening to and caring for. But I would suggest the same should not be true of the withering voice, at least not in the long run. That voice was a sort of construct, a sort of Frankenstein creature, an amalgam of the attitudes of parents and others. John needed to listen to what this voice had to say but only in order that its oppressive power might be challenged. In the end it was not really him at all, though for a time it had usurped some of John's own power and energy. But at the kingdom banquet it will surely not have a place. It will itself have withered, and its energy will be available for more fruitful use.

In what I am saying, I am particularly pointing to the importance of 'the least of these' finding a place at the table and being listened to and cared for. Often this will be some aspect of your inner child of the past, the hurt, unloved, frightened child you once were, and whose feelings can still surface unbidden in certain situations even sixty years later. I think for example of a woman who was sexually abused by a relative when she was a teenager. For her 'the least of these' is herself at sixteen. For another it is the bespectacled and bullied schoolboy he once was, and in certain situations feels that he still is. For another, like the very clever woman I mentioned earlier, 'the least of these' may not be particularly associated with childhood at all, more with an aspect of your character. But whatever form it takes, it is particularly the least of these that is to be given a special invitation, is to be brought particularly within the ambit of God's love and care. It is the least of these who has a very special place in the heart of God.

After one retreat when I had used the words from Mark 1, quoted at the beginning of this chapter, someone wrote to me: 'The thought that God could delight in me as a baby, a small child, an adolescent and an adult makes up for years of feeling rejected and unwanted as a child.' I had not in fact suggested applying the words in that way. That was simply how that person had used them, obviously to some good effect.

I suppose none of us reaches adulthood without some emotional wounds and disabilities. All of us need a lot of appropriate loving and nurturing to catch up with our humanity again and so that our giftedness may be more freely at God's disposal. Let me end this chapter as I began it with some words from Julian of Norwich:

> As truly as God is our Father, so just as truly is he our Mother. In our Father, God Almighty, we have our being; in our merciful Mother we are remade and

restored. Our fragmented lives are knit together and perfected. And by giving and yielding ourselves, through grace, to the Holy Spirit we are made whole. (*Revelations of Divine Love*, chs 59, 58).

AN EXERCISE

Reflect for a little about who is 'the least of these' in your own nature, that aspect of yourself that you most want to disown. Think of that set of feelings or that aspect of your character as though he or she were a person. Spend a few minutes writing a brief character sketch of him or her. Allow your imagination to visualise him or her. If you like, draw him or her. (Possibly an old photo of yourself might help to crystallise your awareness of this aspect of your nature.)

Then do a meditation in the way described in Chapter 6, using Mark 10:13–16. When you have watched the various people bringing their children to Jesus, bring your own 'least of these' to him, for him to touch and to love. You might also like to bring to him other members of your inner population.

If you find this helpful, you might use the last part of this meditation on a number of occasions, and come back to it especially when you feel tempted to disown your 'least of these'.

For further reflection
As in the course of time you open your deeper self to God, do not be dismayed by feelings of profound unworthiness or sinfulness that may surface. They are natural and to be expected as you allow God closer; for God is God, and not just a human friend or lover. Do not resist them. There is a sense in which you *are* nothing in comparison with God. But you are also deeply loved and accepted, beyond anything that human beings are capable of.

Know yourself to be loved through and through . . .

THE VELVETEEN RABBIT

The Skin Horse had lived longer in the nursery than any of the others. He was so old that his brown coat was bald in patches and showed the seams underneath . . . 'What is REAL?' asked the Rabbit one day, when they were lying side by side near the nursery fender, before Nana came to tidy the room. 'Does it mean having things that buzz inside you and a stick-out handle?'

'Real isn't how you are made,' said the Skin Horse. 'It's a thing that happens to you. When a child loves you for a long, long time, not just to play with, but REALLY loves you, then you become Real.'

'Does it hurt?' asked the Rabbit.

'Sometimes,' said the Skin Horse, for he was always truthful. 'When you are Real you don't mind being hurt.'

'Does it happen all at once, like being wound up,' he asked, 'or bit by bit?'

'It doesn't happen all at once,' said the Skin Horse. 'You become. It takes a long time . . . Generally, by the time you are Real, most of your hair has been loved off, and your eyes drop out and you get loose in the joints and very shabby. But these things don't matter at all, because once you are Real you can't be ugly, except to people who don't understand.'

'I suppose *you* are Real?' said the Rabbit. And then he wished he had not said it, for he thought the Skin Horse might be sensitive. But the Skin Horse only smiled.

'The Boy's Uncle made me Real,' he said. 'That was a great many years ago; but once you are Real you can't become unreal again. It lasts for always.'

The Rabbit sighed. He thought it would be a long time before this magic called Real happened to him. He longed to become Real, to know what it felt like; and yet the idea of growing shabby and losing his eyes and whiskers was rather sad. He wished that he could become it without these uncomfortable things happening to him. (Margery Williams, *The Velveteen Rabbit*, Heinemann, 1922, pp. 14–16)

Know Your Gifts and Leanings

'Gifts' is a word that has a high-flying flavour. If you are told that someone is gifted you expect to find they have some exceptional talent for singing songs or designing clothes or inventing electronic wizardry. 'Gifted children' are those with extra special abilities in, say, maths or playing the violin. The word tends to have artistic or intellectual connotations, and always conveys that there is something out of the ordinary about the person who has a gift.

The first thing I want to do is to get away from both those notions. I believe there are many more gifts than those associated with the arts or with thinking: and everyone has gifts, they are not confined to the exceptional few. Here are the beginnings of a wider list of talents:

accept	advise	arrange
clarify	communicate	commit myself
construct, build	co-operate	create
design	display	draw
do precision work	enable	encourage
envision	inspire	interpret
invent	lead	learn
listen	love	negotiate
observe	paint	perform

play	read	reconcile
repair	research	search
sing	speak	supervise
teach	think	write

These are verbs, because talents are expressed in action. But some are more easily expressed as adjectives, for example:

adventurous	clearheaded	compassionate
down to earth	gentle	hospitable
humorous	intuitive	open to God
playful	perceptive	practical
receptive	spontaneous	wholehearted

If you think about some of the things you have done or achieved in your life which have given you particular satisfaction, you could look through this list and see which talents you used in those activities. It is not by any means intended to be a complete list; it is more of a starter to get you thinking about this topic. You could no doubt add to it and you might want to alter it. But it does, I hope, have the advantage of broadening the notion of what gifts might be.

But even a list like that, however amplified and expanded, will never quite do justice to the infinitely subtle variety of human giftedness, because gifts are not so much something you have or something you possess. In the end they are very much bound up with what you *are* as a person. Rather than saying that everyone *has* gifts it might be truer to say that everyone potentially *is* a gift to others. And the characteristics of the gift that you could be are bound up with your own personal characteristics and your history, your abilities and also your disabilities. Disabilities are often crucial in this matter. In fact for some of us our giftedness is particularly released through coming to terms with our disabilities.

Basically the exercising of your gift is the enactment of yourself. Kahlil Gibran expresses it with great beauty and poetry:

You give but little when you give of your possessions.
It is when you give of yourself that you truly give . . .
There are those who give little of the much which
they have – and they give it for recognition and their
hidden desire makes their gifts unwholesome.
And there are those who have little and give it all.
These are the believers in life and the bounty of life,
and their coffer is never empty . . .
And there are those who give and know not pain
in giving, nor do they seek joy, nor give with mindful-
ness of virtue;
They give as in yonder valley the myrtle breathes
its fragrance into space.
Through the hands of such as these God speaks,
and from behind their eyes He smiles upon the earth.
(*The Prophet*, Heinemann, 1926, pp. 24–7)

I wonder how you feel when I suggest that everyone has
a gift? Perhaps you are aware of yours and exercise it.
Maybe you are aware of many gifts within you, only some
of which you use. Or like very many people you may feel
you have no gifts at all, as though the word simply does
not apply to people like you. A friend remarked that she
was afraid to think about the possibility that she might
have gifts: 'It's safer not to look rather than look and
find nothing there.' Certainly one of the main factors that
prevents people identifying and using their gifts is low
self-esteem. Elizabeth O'Connor goes as far as to call it a
raging disease of our time (*Letters to Scattered Pilgrims*, p.
112). That is one reason why the theme of the last chapter
is such an important factor in the search for your personal
calling. The knowledge that you are loved by God, leading
to appropriate self-love, is vital if you are to be able to give
of yourself fully and generously. Without that, you are
likely to undervalue yourself and that is like trying to run
with a ball and chain attached to your ankle. Many of us
are not free of this even when we have done quite a bit of
work on it, and need daily to open ourselves to God's love.
Here is a text for us: 'My daughter, in all modesty, keep

your self respect and value yourself at your true worth. Who will speak up for a woman who is her own enemy, or respect one who disparages herself?' (Ecclus. 10:28–29). The original writer expressed it in terms of 'my son'. I have changed the gender because generally speaking women are even more afflicted in this way than men are because of the way society has regarded women.

If low self-esteem is the main obstacle to *discovering* your giftedness, there are obstacles also to *exercising* your gifts, as you become more aware of them. Sometimes when working with groups I have asked them briefly to list the things that hold them back. Some typical ones are:

'I'm afraid of sticking my neck out.'
'I don't know enough.'
'I'm afraid of failing.'
'I'm too lazy.'
'I'm too busy with other commitments.'
'I'd feel too exposed.'
'People might think I'm pushy or big-headed.'
'It's too risky.'
'I'm afraid of opposition and criticism.'
'I don't know how to begin.'
'I'm afraid of making a fool of myself.'
'I would prefer to be asked.'

Those are some common reasons for hanging back. Up to a point they are realistic. You may well encounter opposition and criticism. There may well be times when you feel that you are out there on your own. You may fail, in the world's estimation as well as in your own. You may indeed have a lot to learn. Ask anyone who has begun to be generous with their gifts whether these kind of feelings are their experience and I guess most will agree. But if you ask them whether they have had cause to regret what they have done they will tell you 'not for one moment'. They had a whale of a time. In spite of the difficulties, in spite of the fact that they did not feel they had much to show for it, they had a ball, because of that deep sense that they were doing what they were born to do.

Another obstacle to exercising your gift is the fear of others' envy. That is a realistic fear too. Elizabeth O'Connor writes: 'As for the exercising of gifts, let everyone be cautious. The exercising of gifts evokes envy – makes enemies of those who, if you stay commonplace, would be your friends' (*Eighth Day of Creation*, p. 74). Envy can lead to us ever so subtly standing in someone's way, or discouraging them, or maligning them and running them down. The reason is always because we are not exercising our own gifts fully enough. That is the root of this kind of malice. It is true to say that it is impossible to give genuine encouragement to another person in the exercise of their gift unless you are also finding joy and freedom in enacting your own gift. The best way of setting others free to live their gifts is by having a great time enacting your own. As Gordon Cosby says:

> We are not sent into the world in order to make people good. We are not sent to encourage them to do their duty. The reason people have resisted the Gospel is that we have gone out to make people good, to help them to do their duty, to impose new burdens on them, rather than calling forth the gift which is the essence of the person himself.

He goes on to say that we do this basically by exercising our own gifts:

> The person who is having the time of his life doing what he is doing has a way of calling forth the deeps of another. Such a person is good news. He is not *saying* the good news. He *is* the good news. He is the embodiment of the freedom of the new humanity. (quoted in Elizabeth O'Connor, *Journey Inward, Journey Outward*, Harper & Row, 1968, pp. 36–7)

Envy raises its ugly head when we are not doing what we are for. But although it can engender really mean and malicious behaviour it also has a positive side; it *can* be a clue to your unlived gifts. So it is worth spending a little time on it now, rather than consigning it to the dustbin without further thought. For practical purposes envy wears three faces. The first is relatively superficial. If someone tells me they have had a holiday in the Alps I feel 'very envious'. I love the Alps and long to go again some day, but it is not a longing that affects my life deeply or widely. I would say that is an example of surface envy.

The second face of envy is deep. The Seekers, a folk group of the sixties, had a song about a rich man's daughter standing at her window and watching the lovers walk by hand in hand, and she sings: 'They see the diamonds I wear, but not the tears of envy in my eyes'; and the chorus goes: 'When will the good apples fall on my side of the fence, when will I taste the sweet fruits of love?' This is the longing for relatedness in every human heart and when it is not fulfilled to some degree in some form, then there is a painful envy of other people's friendships, other people's marriages, other people's closeness. Here the envy is the unsatisfied longing for relatedness and that can be very painful indeed. But even this can have a positive side when it moves you to a more active search for relatedness. Another aspect of this face of envy is the envy of others' status or possessions. The root of this is an inner sense of being unvalued and unappreciated. If unacknowledged and unmet, this kind of envy can be the very devil.

But it is the third face of envy which interests me most, and which potentially has the most positive aspect. When I resigned my parish at the end of 1981 the project for which I now work was little more than a gleam in my eye. I used sometimes to read the advertisements in the *Church Times* and whenever I saw a notice of a retreat I would feel a little pang of envy. I knew it was because I was not at that time doing retreats myself which, if you understand me, I should have been doing. It was not a 'should' from anyone else. It was a 'should' from the heart of my own being, a little nudge from the pit of my stomach that whispered, if I cared to listen: 'That is what *you* are for.'

I began to try to write this book early in 1985, and had considerable difficulty in getting started. During that time I went into a bookshop in Durham and saw Gerard

W. Hughes' book, *God of Surprises*. I picked it up and began
idly looking at the chapter headings and noticed things
like 'Beginning to dig for the treasure' and 'Recognising
the treasure when you find it'. My immediate thought was
'He's written my book!' When I had got over the initial
shock, I realised what it was telling me. Something within
me to be written was struggling to get out, as my envy
would not let me forget. In the end I realised I would only
feel he had written my book if I did not find the courage
to write it myself.

In other words this kind of envy, the envy of someone
else's activity, is a clue to your own potential, a sign of
what you are capable of but are not doing, or at least not
full-bloodedly enough. It is not a spur to imitation, it is a
clue, and often no more than a clue, to your own unlived
energy. For me it was a tussle between envy and fearful-
ness. Envy and longing drive you on, fear and indolence
hold you back, for the tasks to which God calls you always
feel beyond your powers.

So envy can be a clue to what I should be doing in the
sense of 'should' I described earlier. If I act on it I experience an upsurge of energy and enthusiasm for the task.
But I may allow it to have the opposite effect. I may shirk
the struggle. In that case my envy is liable to turn destructive. It seems to be a kind of law of our spiritual life as
human beings that if we are not doing what we are for in
some degree, we devalue and downgrade and generally
discourage the efforts of others, especially when they are
beginning to do what they are for. Envy may have its
positive side. At its worst it is murderously destructive of
love and creativity.

Before we go on to the exercise which I hope will help
you to be a bit more aware of your own gifts, there are
two points I want to make. The first is about the relationship between gifts and call. It may seem as though I have
assumed that if you know what your gift is you automatically know what God wants you to do with it. But that is
by no means always the case, even though the two are
very much connected. For example, if I become aware that

I have a gift for writing, that when I write generously it seems to communicate with people, that does not tell me *what* the Lord wants me to write; should it be articles for *Reader's Digest* or novels or radio plays or newspaper articles, or should I start a parish magazine for my local church, or what? That is a matter of 'hearing' what God is calling you to. We will try and look more directly at that in Chapter 13, though the topics of every chapter have a bearing on it, as explained in Chapter 1.

Secondly it will, I hope, have become clear that when I speak of gifts I am using the word in the widest possible sense. In some Christian circles when you speak of gifts it is assumed you mean those mentioned in St Paul's lists in Romans 12, 1 Corinthians 12, and Ephesians 4. But as St Paul himself makes clear, the gifts he is talking about are ones that are necessary for building up the community of the church. They are what one might call inward journey gifts, gifts required for nurturing the inner life of church communities. In no sense are they intended as a comprehensive list of gifts. Nor of course are they the only sort given by God. All human giftedness is God-given.

AN EXERCISE

Think of people you admire. They could be people you know personally, well-known people, people from history, TV characters, fictional characters, anyone. Make a list of the qualities you admire and the activities or actions that you admire.

What you now have is a list of your own undeveloped or under-developed capacities. Does that surprise you? I do not mean that you are potentially a clone of the person you admire. I mean that the fact that you admire a particular quality or activity means that you too have some capacity for it, or at any rate more than you are at present exhibiting. So it is important to focus on particular qualities or activities, rather than the whole character of the person. Rarely will you find that you admire everything about a person, so it is important to be aware of the specific qualities or doings which your admiration focuses on.

Sometimes when offered this exercise people have difficulty believing it can be a clue to their own gifts. But try it before you come to too hasty a conclusion. It is based on the principle of projection, which is more commonly taken in a negative sense; that is, the common – and often correct – view that the faults that you find particularly irritating in others are ones you are guilty of yourself. But it is a principle that is also valid in a positive sense, as I am suggesting. To paraphrase Sir Thomas Browne's words, 'we carry within us the wonders we seek without us'. (*Religio Medici*, pt. 1, 15)

If you are sharing with a group
There is a further exercise you could do in a group. First have some quiet. Then make a list of things you particularly enjoy doing, things that make you feel more alive and energised, things you have done that you are proud of or that you feel good about. They need not be things that others have valued or even noticed – just things that give you satisfaction. Each person then chooses three that they would be willing to talk about. Allow 15 minutes for this.

For the next stage you will need pencils and small pieces of paper. I am supposing that it is a group of four people, A, B, C and D. First A has a turn at talking about his three activities. The others listen and where necessary encourage A to express his enthusiasm and interest; find out what he enjoys about these activities, what is involved in doing them, and so on. As he speaks each of the others jots down the gifts and qualities they see in A as he talks. If you have the list from the beginning of this chapter at the back of your mind *do not be limited by it*. Be open to notice what you can about A's talents as he speaks. In other words listen to him, not the list! Seven minutes should be enough for this.

Then B reads out each of the talents she has noticed in A. Do not read them like a shopping list; say each one directly to A, looking him in the eye, for example 'I see in you a capacity for . . .'. Mention each talent in this kind of way. Then B gives her list to A, then C and D also read theirs out and give them to A. If C and D have seen some of the same things as B, do not omit them. A can then have a chance to react if he likes, but try to avoid dismissing what the others have said. Let A simply receive them and resist the temptation to depreciate them or play them down! He might also say which ones surprised him most and which ones he liked hearing most. Allow 7 minutes for this.

Then B, C and D each have the same opportunity in turn (a total of 15 minutes each).

When you have done this exercise, which will take an hour and a quarter, keep the lists the others have given you and put them in your journal. They are not a complete list of your gifts. They do not define you once and for all. Another group might see different capacities in you. But let them be an aid to helping you to own your God-given capacities and talents.

(Based on an exercise in J. McMakin and R. Nary, *Doorways to Christian Growth*, Winston Press, 1984, pp. 198–9.)

BURIED TREASURE

Several hundred years ago an obscure Jewish rabbi, Isaac son of Jekel, lived in great poverty in Cracow. One night he had a vivid dream about a treasure buried beneath the bridge leading to the royal castle at Prague. Three nights running he dreamt the same dream, and decided to make the long journey to Prague on foot. At length, footsore and weary, he found the bridge. Imagine his disappointment when he discovered that it was closed to the public and that there were guards on duty night and day. As he hung about wondering what to do next, the captain of the guard noticed him and asked him if he had lost something. Whereupon the rabbi told him about the dream. The officer laughed: 'You don't want to take any notice of dreams,' he cried. 'Why, only the other night I had a dream about a treasure – buried behind the stove in the house of some

rabbi in Cracow by the name of Isaac. But no one in their
right mind pays any attention to dreams.' The rabbi listened with inward astonishment. He bowed low and
thanked the officer for his interest and made off as quickly
as he could back to Cracow. He dug in the neglected corner
of his house and found the treasure, which put an end to
his poverty. (adapted from Mircea Eliade, *Myths, Dreams
and Mysteries*, Harvill Press, 1960, pp. 244–5)

11

Know the World's Needs, Feel the World's Pain

I have devoted much space in these pages to the inward dimension of our life. I have stressed the importance of action coming from within you and not merely being reaction to the expectations and demands of others. This approach could easily be taken to convey that God's calling arises solely within you. But the only reason I have given such emphasis to the inner dimension is because of the strongly other-determined nature of the culture we live in, which I pointed to in Chapter 2. It is not that the outer dimension is unimportant but that it should not be allowed to obscure the inner one. I believe that because of the kind of society and culture we live in there needs to be some positive discrimination in favour of the inner one if this is not to happen. Hence the emphasis I have given to it. The calling of God, however, does not only arise from within. At its most basic the calling of God involves three elements – God, you, and the world's needs. We need to give some attention now to the third of those three.

God's calling to us is in most cases to engage with the world's need. I say 'in most cases' because there are people whose calling is not in any obvious sense 'for' anyone. 'They give as in yonder valley the myrtle breathes its fragrance into space.' That is obviously true of artists, composers, writers, and contemplatives. 'I have never bothered or asked in what way I was useful to society as a whole,' Goethe wrote to a friend, 'I contented myself with expressing what I recognised as good and true.' Though he did add, 'that has certainly been useful in a wide circle; but that was not the aim; it was the necessary result' (quoted by J. Pieper in *Leisure – the Basis of Culture*, p. 37). In some cases perhaps, the enrichment of others is a by-product rather than the conscious intention. For most of us the tasks God calls us to undertake bring us into direct contact with people and are therefore more obviously 'for' particular people, the pensioners in our parish or the jobless in our district; or they focus on some particular issue like housing or the environment.

There is an obvious danger in doing things *for* a particular group of people, which is expressed in Oscar Wilde's dictum: 'There are those who do good, and those who have good done to them. You can recognise the latter by their hunted look.' Unless we are continually engaging in the inward journey in the kind of way I have been describing we run the risk of being meddlesome do-gooders whose actions serve mainly ourselves and our egos. Unless we act out of the secure knowledge that we are loved, we are liable to use our activities to bolster our self-esteem. Unless what we do is a generous and unselfregarding enactment of our gifts, we risk using the people we purport to serve to gain a spurious sense of our own importance.

But, though there are exceptions, God does call most of us to tasks that are for others in some recognisable way. So it is important that we take the time and trouble to be informed about our world, about how people live, about the many ways in which their lives are impoverished, about what imprisons people and narrows their opportunities, about how incredibly blind we can be to what diminishes and oppresses whole sections of the human race. Otherwise we shall either be deaf to people's needs or we shall be acting according to our fantasies – our assumptions about what their needs are.

One or two examples might help here. Last year 'Beth' wanted to train as a volunteer in an advice centre in a northern town. She was to start her training by spending a month observing while sitting in with an experienced worker. She was academically able and had some experience in counselling. She came from a family that was actively involved in left-of-centre politics and she would have said that she was well-informed about such issues as poverty and unemployment. However it was obvious on her first morning that she was very disturbed by what she was seeing and hearing. On three occasions she left the room with some excuse. After the session in which they saw about fifteen people she and the worker sat down for a chat and a cup of coffee. The conversation proceeded as follows:

'What did you think of this morning's session?'

'It was horrific. Although I've read a lot about poverty I had no idea it was like this. Is it always this bad?'

'That was a very average morning, in no way unusual.'

'But what about that family who had no electricity? How can she possibly manage with the children, with no washing machine, no lights or television?'

'The family has no television or washing machine.'

'That's ridiculous! Everyone has these things.'

'Few people in this area have these things.'

'If they are unable to pay the electricity, why don't they pay through standing order or see their bank manager?'

'They don't have a bank account and have never had one. No bank manager would open one for people in their position.'

It is not difficult to understand why she was so shocked and upset. This person went on to train as an advice worker but spent many hours dealing with her own attitudes and fantasies about people living on benefit. Often being exposed to poverty is very different from reading about it. I remember when I first went to Sunderland as a parish priest the policy of the parish was against having jumble sales to raise money for the church. One woman in the congregation told me rather firmly that jumble sales were essential; for many people it was the only way they could afford to clothe their families. From then on she did a good job organising regular jumble sales, though not as a way of raising church funds.

Beth may sound unusually distanced from poverty because of her middle-class background and assumptions. 'Janet' came from a working-class family, married someone with a well-paid job and joined the ranks of the home owners. She remembers her family were very poor in the war years, but she has left all that behind:

'It's not like that now. People can get state benefits. They've all got videos and they can afford to smoke and go out drinking. They are not poor like we were. It's just that they can't budget properly.'

One Lent a fellow church member in her parish organised a series of meetings under the title 'Know your community'. It is a parish that includes a wide cross-section of people, being about two-thirds council estate and one-third private housing. The organiser had taken care to choose a broad social mix for the group. They were keen to learn more about their parish and also to gain some understanding of each other and each other's lifestyle, so they arranged to meet every week in a different house. By the end Janet's attitude had noticeably softened, as had some of the others'.

'I've wept at some of the despair I've seen,' she said. 'When we were poor, everyone was in the same position. Now, with television the differences are much more obvious. It must feel terrible if you can't give your children what most other children have. I was reminded of my daughter when she was young. One day she brought home a friend. She could tell by my face that I was shocked by her shabby appearance and she looked at me and said, "Mummy, she's lovely on the inside." I'll never forget that.'

Some ignorance, like Beth's, is plain lack of knowledge. She had plenty of goodwill but was ill-informed. Much more often, like Janet, we are wilfully ignorant. We do not want to know about the poor. If we knew it would make us feel guilty and uncomfortable, so we pretend that it is not happening, that it cannot happen now in our country. And the press, mostly, gladly reinforces our prejudices and tells us what we want to hear. Otherwise we would not buy newspapers.

Is that unfair to the press? You may remember in 1984 the famous case of the bishop and the shoes, when the Bishop of Durham told the General Synod of the Church of England about the Sunderland family in which the two boys went to school by turns because they only had one pair of shoes between them. The media, and even members of the government, indulged in the most incredible antics to make the bishop look a fool or a liar. The agency which gave him his information deals with cases of poverty every day, year in and year out. In the days that followed his speech the staff were besieged day and night by reporters wanting to know the identity of the family so that the story could be discredited as exceptional or phoney. But no newspaper nor television nor radio ever mentioned the fact, *which reporters were explicitly given*, that on that particular day the agency had twenty-two families on its books who were in a similar position. We, the public, would not have wanted to hear it: we are decent people and it might have disturbed our peace of mind. If we took it too seriously it might have implications for the level of taxes that we pay.

Poverty is one issue which raises passions that we prefer to let sleep. Nuclear weaponry is another which arouses strong feelings of many kinds. Joanna Macey draws attention to one kind in particular; the deep despair that the possibility of a nuclear holocaust produces. She is an American ex-school-teacher who now travels about the world doing what she calls Despair and Empowerment Workshops. She maintains that the main force which keeps most of us apathetic and ignorant about the nuclear question is the very deep despair that a normal human being feels about it – that is, if he allows himself to feel at all. Most of us do not. We prefer to exist in a kind of numbness which keeps the despair feelings at bay. But those feelings are not too far to seek. Joanna Macey lists some of the off-the-cuff comments that people make when the possibility of nuclear war is mentioned:

'It's too horrible to think about. I just block it out.'
'If I don't think about it, maybe it won't happen.'
'Everything I do seems pointless. It could all go at any time.'
'Maybe it won't land here. Maybe we'll survive.'
'It won't ever be dropped. No one's that crazy.'
'If it happens, it happens. I just hope it's quick.'
(*Despair and Personal Power in a Nuclear Age*, New Society Publishers, 1983, p. 5)

She quotes the observation of a participant in one of her workshops:

My name is Mark. I work on contract to the navy, consulting on weapons systems. This week my little boy was sorting books for a school sale, and asked if he should keep some of his favourites to pass on to his own children. I could hardly answer because I realised that I doubted whether he would live that long. (ibid, pp. 93–4)

If poverty raises our sense of guilt and fears for our own prosperity, the possibility of a nuclear holocaust engenders despair; and rightly so. It is not a sick or a neurotic response. It is the natural response of a living, loving human being to such a horrific possibility. In one of his speeches Martin Luther King remarked that in many people's opinion the most important thing in life is to be well-adjusted and not neurotic. He went on, 'But I say to you, there are certain things within our social order to which I am proud to be maladjusted and to which I call upon all men of good will to be maladjusted' (*Testament of Hope*, ed. J. M. Washington, p. 216). Joanna Macey's workshops are designed on the assumption that we can only begin to deal with the nuclear issue constructively and actively by being willing to face and to feel our despair, and by moving through it to rediscover our blocked energy and motivation. Otherwise we blank off our feelings and convince ourselves that we are powerless to do anything anyway.

Her thesis could be applied more widely than just to the nuclear weapons issue. There are many other threats to life on our planet – toxic waste, radioactivity, loss of forest land, plant and animal life facing extinction, food additives and contamination, torture and unjust detention, to say nothing of the economic greed that imposes hunger and poverty on large sections of the world's population. There is a high level of what she calls 'planetary distress'.

That was how things looked in the mid-1980s when I was writing this book. In 1999, as I prepare a new edition, the nuclear threat has receded somewhat – though it could return very quickly if a terrorist organisation got hold of nuclear weapons. At the present moment threats to the environment are more at the centre of people's awareness.

I have probably said enough, perhaps more than enough, to make the first two of the three very limited points that I want to make in this chapter. The first is that if we are to be generous with our gifts and energies we need to be well-informed, to listen to news, read books and articles, take an interest in current affairs, read newspapers. We need to be aware of how the media slant their reporting and why. We need to have some understanding of people's real needs if our activities are not to be misplaced. This is not as straightforward as it sounds. 'A man's eyes', says one of Charles Kingsley's characters in a discussion of poverty, 'can only see what they've learnt to see.' The quotation is used by K. S. Inglis (*Churches and the Working Classes in Victorian England*, Routledge, 1963, p. 250). He continues:

For most of the nineteenth century, Englishmen looked at poverty and found it morally tolerable because their eyes were trained by evangelical religion and political economy. A preacher could spend his life surrounded by the squalor of a manufacturing town without feeling any twinge of socially radical sentiment, when he believed that many poor people were suffering for their own sins, and that the plight of the rest was the result of spiritual ordinances which it would be impious to question and of economic laws which it was foolish to resist; charity could alleviate the suffering caused by these laws, but in any case the poor had only to wait until death for the end of all temporal hardships and distinctions. Many men who believed these things were humane; but pity alone would never provide them with an alternative social theory.

This vision of poverty was shared by many who would not have admitted that evangelical religion influenced them. The Tractarians, despite their theological revolt against evangelicalism, still saw the poor as individual souls to be saved and not as members of a society to be transformed. Drastic mental changes were necessary before the eyes of a Christian could learn to see poverty differently.

I have used the example of poverty: but of course it is true in other spheres. We see the world and other people through the spectacles of our mental constructs. There is a great need for humility in being willing to admit this and be open to seeing it more nearly as it is. There is also a need to be clear-eyed about the operation of power and self-interest in our society. Things do not change because enough people with enough power have a lot to lose.

The second point is that if we are to know the needs of the world we must open our hearts to feel its pain. No amount of information will have the slightest effect if, as St John puts it, our hearts (literally, guts) are closed (1 John 3:17). But to begin to open them is quite demanding (there is a tape 'Open to the world's pain', available from the address on p. 207), and once again it can be a great help to have the support of others or of a group. It is perhaps worth adding that in opening your heart and your feelings to the world's pain you are not thereby committed to taking *all* the responsibility for action upon yourself. That is one of the fears that can get in the way. One thing that can deter us from feeling the world's distress is that we assume that feeling it somehow makes us responsible for trying to 'solve it'. But in fact God only asks each one to undertake a tiny part of the global task. The first step is to open your heart; it is then a further step to become aware of what part of the action is yours.

The third point concerns the sphere or the method of the activity which you offer. Because what I am saying in this book starts with the individual, you may have formed the impression that any action that might ensue would be isolated and individual, perhaps even limited to personal acts of charity such as Professor Inglis describes. I have certainly been at pains to stress the importance of finding your own personal energy and enthusiasm. That is the strongest motive power for getting things done, whether you are on your own or with others. But the initiative that you take will in many cases be at work, or in the context of an institution such as a local church or voluntary organisation, or in politics or some other sphere where only if there are to be changes in the social structure will people be enabled to find new life and to flourish. Though what I am pointing to will always be in some sense a personal initiative, it may well consist of trying to influence or change the way an existing institution works, rather than starting a new one. Changing an existing institution or social structure is a much more difficult and demanding task than starting something fresh (though of course the latter *can* be an effective means to the former end). So the importance of this kind of activity cannot be over-estimated, and this point is made by the parable at the end of this chapter. It is not that personal and individual activity is ruled out. I am simply making the obvious point that if that is the *only* sphere where we expect to hear God's call, then huge tracts of institutional and political life are left out of account. I do not believe that they are of no consequence to the coming of the kingdom. After all we are bidden to pray: 'Your kingdom come, your will be done, *on earth* as it is in heaven.'

AN EXERCISE

Visit somewhere you have never been before and spend half an hour just observing quietly and noticing as much as you can. Here are some ideas of places to go to:

advice centre
bus journey round town
bus station
council in session
court room
hospital casualty department
industrial firm
Job Centre
centre for people with
  learning disabilities
club/disco/bar
old people's home

playgroup/toddler group
political meeting
prison or detention centre
school playground
shopping centre
welfare benefits office
Student Union building
Tenants' Association meeting
theatre/cinema foyer

walk in a part of the town
  that is unfamiliar to you

Perhaps do two or three different visits. You may have ideas of your own to add to the list, but let them be situations that are unfamiliar to you. As you do these visits there is no reason why you should not speak to people if you wish, but be clear that the aim is to observe and listen, to open your eyes and ears.

After each visit reflect in your journal about your contemplative visit. Use the following questions as a guide:

Where did you see stress or distress on someone's face?
What do you think is causing it?
Did you see people imprisoned or enslaved?
What do you think is the cause?
In what ways are people you have seen today impoverished or blind? What do you think is the cause?
What would constitute good news, or release, or sight for these people?
Where did you see interest or enthusiasm or joy or celebration?
How could you be better informed about the experiences and circumstances of the people you have seen today and about the institutions and forces that shape their lives?
What might God be saying to you in all this?

(An additional exercise for use with this chapter is available on a cassette tape. See page 207.)

A PARABLE

There was once a factory which employed thousands of people. Its production line was a miracle of modern engineering, turning out thousands of machines every day. The factory had a high accident rate. The complicated machinery of the production line took little account of human error, forgetfulness or ignorance. Day after day people came out of the factory with squashed fingers, cuts, bruises. Sometimes a worker would lose an arm or a leg. Occasionally someone was electrocuted or crushed to death.

Enlightened people began to see that something needed to be done. First on the scene were the churches. An enterprising minister organised a small first aid tent outside the factory gate. Soon with the backing of the Council of Churches it grew into a properly built clinic, able to give first aid to quite serious cases, and to treat minor injuries. The town council became interested, together with local bodies like the Chamber of Trade and the Rotary Club. The clinic grew into a small hospital with modern equipment, an operating theatre and a full-time staff of doctors and nurses. Several lives were saved. Finally the factory management, seeing the good that was being done, and wishing to prove itself enlightened, gave the hospital its official backing, with unrestricted access to the factory, a small annual grant and an ambulance to speed serious cases from workshop to hospital ward.

But year by year, as production increased, the accident rate continued to rise. More and more workers were hurt or maimed. And in spite of everything the hospital could do, more and more people died from the injuries they had received.

Only then did some people begin to ask if it was enough to treat people's injuries, while leaving untouched the machinery that caused them. (Brian Wren)

Dream Dreams

In 1975 when I had been a parish priest in Sunderland for nine years I found myself thinking: 'What we need in the north-east is some kind of Iona, as a visible symbol of the importance of living the journey inward and the journey outward in an integral relationship with each other.' I had never been to Iona; but I gathered that the Iona Community had arisen from experience in Glasgow in the 1930s and that Iona was an ancient holy place whose spiritual power had been brought to life as a place of inner journeying, but with an integral relationship with work in urban Glasgow. So it was to me a powerful symbol of living the double journey.

In the north-east, I reflected from my Anglican standpoint, we had our industrial missions and our social responsibility chaplaincies as symbols of the need for the Church to engage with the problems and opportunities of modern society. And we had our religious communities as symbols of the journey inward. But there was no strong symbol linking the two journeys in any full-blooded way.

So I began to think: 'Wouldn't it be marvellous to have an "Iona" in the north-east, to be able to point to it and to its people and be able to say "that's what I mean by living the two journeys. If you want to understand what it is about, go and see those people."' But I did not talk about it much. And I never for a moment thought of doing anything about it. I just wished someone some day would do something.

Somehow as the years went by that dream would not go away. On the odd occasion when I gave attention to it I found myself weeping with longing, and was surprised at the intensity of my feelings about it. But I still had no idea of doing anything about it. It was only when I went to the Church of the Saviour in Washington, DC, for a month in 1978, that I found myself with people who encouraged the dreaming of dreams, and who pushed me with questions like, 'What are *you* going to do about it; what step can you take yourself in the direction of your dream?' That was frightening. It began to feel dangerously arrogant to connect those sort of dreams with anything *I* might do.

Some find it easy to dream dreams. Many people have a gift for seeing round corners, for envisioning the possibilities in a situation. Others are gifted with being practical, with a very good grasp of the art of the possible, but who find dreaming dreams very difficult. Their practical side keeps on dragging them down to earth again. Whereas the dreamers sometimes have a job keeping their feet on the ground at all! But we need to develop both capacities. Each needs the other. Where there is no vision, people lose heart. Where dreams are ungrounded, we live in a make-believe world.

The starting point of any dreaming is dissatisfaction with things as they are. It is important to nurture our dissatisfaction without merely moaning. Krishnamurti puts it well:

What is important is to be wholly discontented, for such total discontent is the beginning of the initiative which becomes creative as it matures ... so one must have this total discontent – but with joy. Do you understand? One must be wholly discontented, not complainingly, but with joy, with gaiety, with love. (quoted in Elizabeth O'Connor, *Eighth Day of Creation*, Word Books, 1971, p. 98)

Where there is no vision, people lose heart

Most discontented people are the most awful bores. We are always grumbling that things are not as they should be. However well things are going, some of us almost need something to grumble about. It is because we have not worked enough with our own store of left-over anger from the past. And so the steam escapes in little whiffs here and there in the form of niggles and complaints, with perhaps every now and then blowing off about something, usually out of all proportion to its actual significance. But do not despise these angry feelings. Listen to them. Feel them as the natural response to things that happened in your past, and vent them in some harmless way, on paper, or by pounding a cushion, or to God. Then your deeper discontent can be free from personal rancour and bitterness. Keep it alive, writes Krishnamurti, 'with the vitality of joy and great affection. Then that flame of discontent will have an extraordinary significance because it will build, it will create, it will bring new things into being.'

All creativity is of God. It is in the most fundamental nature of God to be creative: 'Behold, I make all things new' (Rev. 21:5) 'Cease to dwell on days gone by and to brood over past history. Here and now I will do a new thing; this moment it will break from the bud' (Isa. 43:18–19); 'O sing to the Lord a new song, for he has done marvellous things' (Ps. 98:1).

And yet you might look at God's world and wonder where all this newness is. There does not seem to be much to show for it. 'After a thousand years of mass, we've got as far as poison gas,' wrote Thomas Hardy bitterly. It is true that many terrible things are done, and some of the very worst of them are perpetrated in the name of religion. Unless we are very conscious of our darker side and own it as ours, humanity's brightest light can cast very deep shadows. But things are not all negative and destructive. Look again at the world; look again at your own country, your own district, the people you know. Where do you see signs of hope? Where do you see green shoots? Where do you discern God's liberating action at work? Sometimes at a workshop we do a 'brainstorm' on this theme simply thinking of examples without discussion and without judging, just as a way of exercising our capacity for seeing signs of hope, which otherwise can atrophy so easily. Here are some examples from a recent one:

Children enthused by a teacher.
A sermon by Archbishop Tutu.
A disabled person deciding for herself whether to go on an overseas trip.
Possibilities for peace in Northern Ireland.
A church group making links with overseas students in a university town.
Psychiatric patients singing one evening at a day centre.

Try it for yourself. Jot down each day some little sign of hope that you see. Somehow we need to make the effort to try to see the world as God sees it, to see it with the eyes of hope, to see it as s/he would have it be, to catch a glimpse of God's kingdom. What is God's dream for the world? If we can begin to glimpse a little of that, perhaps we can begin to discern our tiny part of that dream.

'How lovely on the mountains are the feet of the herald who comes to proclaim shalom and to bring good news' (Isa. 52:7). Shalom, usually translated peace or prosperity, means social wholeness. It is much more positive than absence of conflict, much more corporate than individual flourishing, though it includes both of those. What would it be like for shalom to pervade all human living? Think of it in terms of *personal wholeness*: what do you long for for individuals – integration, self-acceptance, unfettered giftedness generously given? Think of it in *inter-personal* terms: how would it be for shalom to prevail between women and men, what would relationships be like? Imagine some practical examples. Think of it in terms of your *firm or organisation*. What changes are needed for wholeness at your place of work? What needs to happen for it to promote shalom for its staff, its clients, its environment? Think of it in *national* terms: how would it be for us to be one nation, what needs to happen to heal the widening division in our country? Think of it in *inter-*

national terms: think of what peace between nations might
be beyond mere absence of conflict; what needs to change
to move towards international shalom. Think of it in terms
of *religions*: what might shalom be between people of different faiths, what do you hope for here? How would
things be if shalom prevailed between us and *the natural
world*; what needs to happen for us to move towards earth
peace? Think of any situation, from classroom to conurbation, from kitchen sink to international crisis; what is
your hope? How might we move towards wholeness, and
not merely absence of conflict? And what might wholeness
mean in corporate, social terms? In each sphere think of
concrete instances of what you would love to see. If you
find the large-scale view difficult, envision some small
creative initiative.

When you have begun to catch a glimpse of God's dream
for the world, you can perhaps get some clues about what
your part of it is. Where is your heart in all this, where do
you find your interest being kindled? For where your heart
is, there will your energy be aroused.

Perhaps I need to point out here that a dream is not the
same as a plan. The function of a dream is to raise your
eyes from the daily round, to lift you off the tramlines, to
set your feet in a larger room. In my own experience that
seemed to be one of the main functions of the dream
that began to captivate me in the mid-seventies. It certainly
was not a plan. At no time have I remotely seen myself as
a sort of George McLeod rebuilding the Priory on Lindisfarne! In fact to start with it never occurred to me to see
myself at all in relation to that dream.

Nevertheless though a dream is not a plan it usually
contains the seeds of action, even if to an outside observer
the resultant action seems to have little connection with the
dream. We will come back to that in a later chapter. But
beware of taking your dream too literally. That can be quite
a snare. Often a place or a building can begin to crystallise a dream for you. In my limited experience one of the
commonest dreams people have is of starting some kind
of hospitable place, a place of rest or retreat or healing. I

am not sure why this is. It is *possible* that the Lord sees the
need for this kind of thing more than anything else. But I
have a suspicious mind; and if I thought I had a calling of
this kind I would want to work with the question, 'Is it *me*
that wants a hospitable place, a place of rest or healing, a
home for the heart?' There is nothing necessarily wrong if
it is. But if it is, then I need to set about getting my own
needs met, or at least accepted and sufficiently integrated,
before I try and offer this kind of thing to others. In either
case, the dream, the longing, may look very similar: but
the implications for action will be very different. The fact
is that often what the dream reveals first is a need of your
own, for healing, withdrawal, rest, retreat. If that is your
need it should be listened to: it would mean taking steps
towards reorganising your life so that it can be met.
Perhaps only then will you be able to be open and unclut-
tered enough to begin to hear what God is calling you to
offer to others. But here I am primarily wanting to
encourage dreams that pass beyond your personal needs,
even though they may in some sense have their original
roots there.

Some kind of discernment is necessary in evaluating the
significance of a dream, in order to see whether it is pointing primarily to your own need or to a wider need. It is
important also to discern the difference between escapist
daydreaming and the kind of dream I have been trying to
point to. When St Ignatius Loyola was a young man he was
badly wounded in his right leg at the siege of Pamplona in
1521. He was forced to spend many boring months confined to the family castle slowly recovering. In those days
even a nobleman's family would not own many books.
Much of the time he spent just sitting enjoying daydreaming about the marvellous deeds he would do to win
the hand of some beautiful woman. But there were one or
two books in the castle including a Life of Christ and some
Lives of the Saints. Some of the time he read these and
found himself daydreaming about all the marvellous
things he would do for Christ and how he would outdo
the saints in his devotion to Jesus. As the time dragged by

he began to notice that although at the time both kinds of daydream were enjoyable, the after-effects seemed to differ. After dreaming of some chivalrous exploit he somehow felt flat and bored and empty. Whereas after dreaming of what he would do for Christ, his interest did not flag; on the contrary he felt energised and hopeful. He was of course eventually to go on to found the Jesuit order. (For a modern exposition of St Ignatius' way of sorting the gold from the dross, see Gerard W. Hughes, *God of Surprises*, pp. 91–103.)

It seems that when a dream is close enough to the 'thread' of your life, you do feel deeply about it. It is not just superficial escapism. Somehow it does not go away. You may not think about it for weeks or months at a time. But when you come back to it, perhaps when you articulate it in talking to someone else or write about it in your journal, you are surprised that somehow it has not faded. Even months or years later it is as fresh as ever and its pull perhaps even stronger. This is one elementary way of distinguishing the two, though of course it needs to be done over a period of time.

I have suggested telling someone else about your dream as a way of noticing how you feel about it. Martin Buber writes:

> When a man grows aware of a new way in which to serve God, he should carry it around with him secretly, and without uttering it, for nine months, as though he were pregnant with it, and let others know of it only at the end of that time, as though it were a birth. (*Ten Rungs*, p. 74)

Dreams should not be spoken of too hastily, and certainly not in the company of people who will not be sensitive to the possible significance to you of what you are saying. It is painfully easy to tread on one another's green shoots. Many people do not understand the function of this kind of dream, and may easily dismiss it on the grounds that it is an unworkable and unpractical *plan*.

But sooner or later it will be important to articulate it in order to help the process of getting it clearer. There does come a time when it is important to rehearse for your own benefit exactly what it is you hope for, never mind how impractical or impossible it may seem. That means being willing to sound foolish and to appear arrogant for daring even to think such thoughts. Here once again we begin to approach the issue of calling, since dreaming dreams is another aspect of the search for God's call to you. A dream on its own is not a call, but it is an important component in the process of listening for what God wants of you. It is a further clue to the treasure that you have to offer.

THREE EXERCISES

1. Jot down your reflections stimulated by the following questions. Give yourself plenty of time for this. Let the questions lie about in your mind at odd moments in the next few days:

- What distresses or worries you most about today's world . . . ?
- Read Luke 4:18–19. . . .
- In today's world, or in your neighbourhood, who are the impoverished . . . ? (Think about this in the widest possible sense. Financial hardship is not the only way in which people are impoverished; think of other kinds of poverty as well.)
- Who are the imprisoned (isolated, shut in, cut off from others physically or because of society's attitudes, etc.) . . . ?
- Who are the blind . . . ?
- Who are the oppressed . . . ?
- In your quieter and more reflective moments, who are the people whose condition touches your heart . . . ?
- What people or issues have concerned you for a long time, perhaps even from when you were much younger . . . ?
- In your reading or watching TV, what topics do you find yourself most interested in or drawn to . . . ?

- In what you see, or what you hear about, what moves you most . . . ?
- What makes you angry in what you see happening . . . ?
- What excites you, fills you with hope and longing for what could be . . . ?
- As you look back over your jottings, notice the people or issues you are particularly drawn to or concerned about. If you were to conceive a hope for them, what would you love to see happen . . . ?
- Write your dream down in as much detail as you can. . . . (e.g. for whom? where? what? how?)

2. An alternative for those who find dreaming difficult
If you could be or do anything you liked in your wildest dreams, what kind of future would you invent for yourself?

Sometimes a person's imagination is bound and cramped by the fear that to dream dreams is selfish or arrogant. Throw off the shackles! Dare to dream dreams for yourself! What in your heart of hearts would you love to do? You do not have to be practical. For this present purpose you can pretend that you have no obligations to family or job, *because the aim is to be in touch with your own inner energy.* The practical questions *must* be left till later if you are to give yourself permission to dream.

3. Another alternative
You have been given only twelve months to live. For ten of those months you will be able to live an active life. How will you spend the time left to you?

The Heart of the Matter

The Lord God said:
I myself will dream a dream within you.
Good dreams come from Me, you know;
My dreams seem impossible, not too practical,

Not for the cautious man or woman;
A little risky sometimes, a trifle brash perhaps;
Some of my friends prefer to rest more comfortably in
sounder sleep with visionless eye.
But for those who share my dreams I ask a little patience,
A little humour, some small courage,
And a listening heart – I will do the rest.
Then they will risk and wonder at their daring,
Run and marvel at their speed,
Build and stand in awe at the beauty of their building.

You will meet me often as you work –
In your companions who share your risk,
In your friends who believe in you enough
To lend their own dreams, their own hands, their own
hearts to your building,
In the people who will find your doorway, stay a while
And walk away knowing that they too can find a dream.
There will be sunfilled days and sometimes it will rain –
A little variety . . .
Both come from Me – so, come, be content;
It is my dream you dream,
It is my house you build,
My caring you witness,
My love you share – and this is the heart of the matter.

(Author unknown)

13

Hear a Call

A church council sits round in a friendly circle: a supportive church this, one that encourages mutual caring and openness in its life. This evening its main item of agenda is to discuss how to express its care and concern for the people of the neighbourhood in which the church is set. So someone puts up a sheet of newsprint and stands ready with felt-tip pen poised: and they begin to list the needs of the locality; the children with nowhere to play, an accident black spot on a main road, vandalism, violence in the home, unemployment, drug addiction, political apathy and so on. Out comes another sheet of newsprint and the list lengthens. And finally there is no spirit left in them, and they fall silent as they gaze at the huge list. The unspoken question that weighs on everyone's mind is, 'How on earth can we few Christians do anything about all that?'

It is important, whether you are on your own or part of a congregation or community, to understand the locality in which you are set and take trouble to be aware of its needs. For a local congregation one of the most valuable things to come out of the *Faith in the City* report all those years ago was the suggestion of a neighbourhood audit for the local church (*Faith in the City*, Church House, 1985, pp. 367–72). I wonder how many actually used it? But when you have done that, you are left with the large and heavy question, 'Which needs do we try to meet and which do we leave unmet?' And if you think of your 'locality' as the nation or the world the question is even larger and heavier.

In practice there is rarely a carefully thought out answer to this. If anything is done at all it is usually because of the enthusiasm of an individual for a particular cause, who sways the others or gathers one or two of them and gets into action. This is not necessarily a bad thing and I believe it provides a clue as to how to approach the unanswered questions more directly and more positively. It all comes down to the need for people to develop their awareness of God's call to them, that individual call which evokes a person's genuine enthusiasm and energy for action.

You might feel that that is not a sufficiently thought out approach; that it is putting too much reliance on individual people's perception of the relative importance of an issue and on what might seem to be the whimsical ways of enthusiasm. My answer to that is threefold.

First it is God who calls. We do not invent our own calls. Ultimately it is God's doing. And I take the view that s/he has things in hand. God knows what needs to be done, and only s/he has the necessary overview of the tasks of the kingdom. There is an appropriate sense in which we must leave the overall plan to God. Our task, *having done all we can to be informed*, is simply to be open to God's call to us.

Secondly listening for God's call involves a good deal of trouble and effort on our side to be open and attentive to what s/he wants of us. It is not just a matter of faddism or short-term enthusiasm. We may not always get it right, but we do need to be prepared to put a lot of care into listening for what s/he wants.

Thirdly I believe that if more of us were responsive to God's call we would feel much less responsible for neglecting the things we are not doing. We would see that other kingdom tasks were being undertaken by other people. There would be less temptation to feel guilty about the tasks which are not ours to do. You are not in fact asked to do it all. To think that you are is a kind of arrogance.

The whole of this book is about putting yourself in the

way of 'hearing' God's personal call to you. If you look
back over the topics and the exercises you will notice that
most of them are about growing in openness, to God, to
ourselves and our potential, and to the world's needs. The
basic issue in all this is to clear away the clutter that
prevents us hearing. God will lead us if only we can discover how to be open enough. Some of the exercises may
not have seemed to be about openness to God. They
may have seemed almost secular. For example, listening to
your feelings may not sound a very godly thing to do,
until you realise that they are a clue to your own God-
given nature and energy. Becoming aware of your gifts
may not seem a very spiritual activity, until you recognise
that they are given to you by God. Doing a course in
sociology or economics or environmental issues may strike
you as the very opposite of a religious activity, until you
remember that unless you take the trouble to be informed
about the world you will be oblivious of the kingdom tasks
waiting to be done.

So now, if you are still with me, we come to reflect more
directly about God's call to you. What does s/he want *you*
to do? What step, however small, is s/he nudging you to
take in the direction of the offering of yourself? That can
be a bit scary to contemplate. At a recent workshop the
participants were asked at the beginning what they hoped
for from the sessions. One person said she wanted to hear
more clearly what God wanted of her; but she confessed
to feeling a bit fearful about what that might be. There
may have been in her mind the shadow of the notion of a
tyrant God. But when all the ghoulish notions of God have
been exorcised, there still remains an appropriate fear when
we open ourselves to God. It is not the abject fear that
s/he might be a slave-driver or a sadist; it is the healthy
and entirely reasonable fear of the unknown. We are afraid
to let go and to let God do what s/he wills with us. For,
as the Book of Isaiah says of God, 'My thoughts are not
your thoughts, and your ways are not my ways . . . For as
the heavens are higher than the earth, so are my ways
higher than your ways and my thoughts than your

thoughts' (Isa. 55:8–9). God's power is likened to fire, God's inscrutability to the wind. Sometimes I think that the Church is designed to keep God at a safe distance, that the things we do in church on a Sunday are ways of keeping God at arm's length because somewhere in our hearts we know that it is dangerous to come too near. It is not surprising that the Church wraps up the notion of calling in ecclesiastical roles (see Chapter 16). It is safer that way. To begin to work with the business of personal calling might turn out to be playing with fire. So let us be clear that it is God who calls, and that our response will always involve a letting go, it will always feel risky; and there will always be something mysterious about how it all works. It will be a source of wonder to us and often of deep joy, but to our minds and our reason it will usually be quite baffling.

It may be that having read so far and having diligently done the exercises you are in any case feeling pretty baffled. Little light may have dawned for you about what God wants of you. There could be three kinds of reasons for this. It may be that you have for so long lived your life by reaction to others' demands that it is going to take much time and patience and struggle to begin to turn your attention within. This might be because of society's expectations or because of your temperament. I have said a little about the former in the earlier part of this book. Here let me say a word about temperament. Some of us are by nature extraverted in the strict sense of the word; that is to say we give priority to outer events. Others are introverted; we give priority to inner events. That is the basic difference between those two temperamental orientations. Some people are able to operate happily in both modes, though most of us tend to lean towards one or the other. But the culture we live in is strongly extraverted in its attitudes. Looking within is discouraged and is sometimes even written off as morbid. So even reading a book like this which is deliberately slanted the other way will be difficult. It will be swimming against the current, particularly for a basically extraverted person. But because of this strong bias in our culture it can be difficult even for someone who is by nature introverted to begin to take their inner life more seriously. For a strongly extraverted person that is a well-nigh impossible task: he will not even see that there is a task to be done! So do not be surprised if progress seems slow. Be patient with yourself and with God.

The second reason might be that fear prevents you opening your mind and heart to God's leading, fear of hurting those close to you, fear of losing what you have – your status in the world, a good standard of living, friends, security, and so on – as well as fear of the unknown and fear of what it might lead to. Those fears may well be crippling unless you have done enough work in the areas described in Chapters 5 to 9. There is no virtue in trying to push yourself through a disabling fear barrier, and faithful and careful work may need to be done before the pathological fears recede enough. But there will still remain a justified and entirely realistic fear. After all, Jesus said, 'Those who want to save their life will lose it, and those who lose their life for my sake will save it. What does it profit them if they gain the whole world at the cost of their true selves?' (Luke 9:24–25). Taking a step, however small, into the unknown will feel risky, and will sometimes be risky. But if you are near enough to the 'thread' of your life, it will also bring you profound inner joy and fulfilment. No outer success is promised, no fame or fortune – probably the opposite – but a great deal of inner satisfaction. And God will be with you, often in very mysterious and unforeseen ways. It may well feel like letting go to the point of foolhardiness, but, says Jesus, it is the road to life.

Some readers will perhaps be waiting for me to say that a third factor that prevents us hearing is sin. Indeed it is, and much of what I have said so far bears that out, even if I have not used the theological word 'sin'. For sin is basically closedness to God. Sin is allowing ourselves to be ruled by the desire for security and status and possessions, allowing our eyes to be blinkered by ignorance, giving in to the fear of offering ourselves and our gifts, and so on – the whole dismal list of things that keep us chained down and prevent us taking wings at God's loving and gracious invitation. That is sin; those are the things that keep us from God and lead us to look for substitutes for real living. If you do not seem to hear a call, it may be that you have settled for a substitute for so long that it is difficult to change.

At this point it might be as well to digress briefly to point to the equal and opposite difficulty, where people claim to have been called by God to tasks which have little to do with furthering the kingdom of love, justice and human flourishing. Peter Sutcliffe, the Yorkshire Ripper, is an example of this. He claimed divine direction to murder prostitutes. Clearly that was the prompting of a diseased mind.

An American founded a cosmetics firm in 1963. Its outlets are through direct sales, where women working on the Tupperware principle are paid on a commission basis. She has successfully raked in the dollars and the company has grown to large proportions by recruiting more and more women. She says, 'God, in his infinite wisdom, had a plan to use my dream company. The first thing we did was to take God as our partner.' She told a sales seminar for six thousand women in Dallas (subtitled Share the Spirit): 'through our company you can become the person God intended you to be'. She promotes the 'go-give spirit', which of course merely means 'get out and sell' (Neil Lyndon, *Sunday Times Magazine*, 16 December 1984). Here the language of religion and personal fulfilment is a device for keeping the sales force motivated.

It is unfortunately the case that 'divine guidance' has been claimed for all kinds of actions, mad or bad or both. In fact the use of that phrase itself alerts us to be suspicious of a person's motivation. Even if someone feels that an opinion or a course of action has been prompted by God, they should be very cautious about making any public claim that it has. Claiming divine guidance puts you – is perhaps intended to put you – above contradiction. It is a claim that we should make very sparingly, because of the danger of arrogance and spiritual blackmail.

How then do you judge whether a call is of God or not? The Society of Friends is one of the few religious denominations to have some system for this which is accessible to any member envisaging action in any sphere, religious or secular.

For the Christian the whole of life is a sphere of service in which he seeks to use his particular gifts to the glory of God. Yet sometimes there may come a leading to some specific task, felt by him as an imperative claim of God upon him not to be denied even if he feels personal reluctance. This is what Friends call a concern, an experience they have known throughout their history. It has been the practice for a Friend, who believes he has heard such a call, to bring his concern before the gathered community of Friends in its monthly meeting, that it may be tested as a true leading of the Spirit. The practice is an expression of our membership with one another, of a mutually accepted obligation, that of the individual Friend to test his concern against the counsel of the group and that of the group to seek the guidance of God in exercising its judgment. (*Church Government*, London Yearly Meeting of the Religious Society of Friends, 1968, para. 861)

The mainline churches have procedures for checking out callings to certain roles like priest or missionary, but not for the kind of personal, creative or innovative call that I have been trying to point to in these pages. I would like to see something like the Quaker system operating in other branches of the Christian Church. A start might be made by a small group in a congregation going through the process I am offering, so that it can offer some sort of confirmation or otherwise of its members' perception of God's calling. I will come back to this in Chapter 16. Otherwise encouraging expectancy about calls is a licence for all kinds of unholy crankery and nuttery, and leaves the way open for the manipulative and even the malicious.

Here however is an attempt at some kind of checklist

for your personal use. Will your projected course of action in some way:

1. be good news for the impoverished?
2. release the imprisoned or oppressed?
3. give sight to the blind?
4. put you on the side of the neglected, or the powerless, or those without a voice?
5. be a generous giving of what you are and of your gifts?
6. be a new departure, a fresh initiative, something not done before, or not in that way?
7. feel risky?
8. be beyond your unaided powers?
9. be a step, however tiny, towards a more just and equitable world?

If your answer is 'yes' to the last five questions and to at least one of the first four that would seem to be pointing in the right sort of direction. I would add four more points.

10. It is likely that it will be something that, basically, you love to do, whatever risk or even suffering it may bring.
11. It is more likely, statistically, to be in the secular sphere than in the church, simply because there is more of it!
12. It is unlikely that it will be full time, at any rate in the early stages. Indeed what you do may be episodic, done in short bursts of time, like evenings or weekends.
13. You will be very fortunate if it is something that you are paid to do.

You might want to add more of your own.

In practice the awareness of a personal call is something that is commoner in middle life than earlier on. For some the first nudgings may come in youth, though at that stage they are usually thought of in terms of a role: 'I want to be a nurse' or 'I want to be an astronaut'. More often it is when you have been working for some years, perhaps in the same job, perhaps bringing up a family, that you begin to be aware of some discontent or vague longings or of actual hints of a new direction. For some this is too much of a threat. It feels too risky even to listen to such seditious whisperings, and the person drowns them by noise, by drink, by hectic activity – anything that helps deafen her or to deaden her awareness. Even if she does give attention to it, it will probably be 'role oriented' to start with for reasons I have explained. It will only become clearer and more differentiated as the person begins to act on such inklings as they have. And it may involve several changes of job or direction as the sense of calling gradually takes more definite shape. In other words it is clarified quite as much by action as by introspection; you discover what you love to do by doing.

Let me give you an example of a friend who is beginning to explore his sense of calling and how it has involved several stages spread over a number of years. We will call him Brian. He was brought up on a council estate in a northern industrial town. When he left school he got an apprenticeship as an engraver in a small firm. He worked for fifteen years in that job. He married and bought his own house and was content in a fairly unreflective way. But much of the time he was on his own at work. If after twelve years or so you had asked him what he would like to do, he would have said he would like to work with people, though he had no idea how or in what capacity. It was about this time that he became a Christian. In the end his discontent reached the point where he left his job and joined a youth and community course at the local poly. Some of his relatives thought he was crazy to throw up a good secure job. The course was a real eye-opener for him in understanding the needs of people in society.

His first job after qualifying was work with young people on a housing estate in a very run-down neighbourhood. He began to be particularly concerned about poverty and the damaging and narrowing effect it has on people. His own background had already given him some personal experience of this. He very much wanted a job that would enable him to work more directly on that issue. He heard of a vacant post for an advice worker at a neighbourhood advice centre on a large housing estate, and was sure that

that would give him the opportunity he needed. He has been working there for several years now dealing with the problems of people on social security or low wages who get into financial difficulties, representing them at tribunals and to officialdom. During that time spare-time opportunities have come his way. He helps with a youth centre. He helps run courses for youth leaders. He is invited to run educational events to inform people about poverty in Britain. He is discovering more and more that what he loves to do is to work with disadvantaged people in groups, helping them to discover their power and their giftedness. And there is no doubt of his considerable ability in that field.

I tell this little bit of his story to illustrate the point that the journey to discovering your personal calling may take you through a series of roles or jobs, each one a bit more suited to your gifts, as you begin to find out in practice what you love to do. But eventually you may discover that the ready-made niches run out. None of them quite fits what you have to offer; none of them really gives you enough freedom to follow up God's unique call to you. And there comes a point where no one is going to hand it to you on a plate. You have got to create your own niche, to take your own initiative unasked. That is really the point at which Brian is. The job for which he is paid does not really give him the opportunities he wants. Is he going to look for another paid job that might give him more of the freedom he seeks? Or is paid work for him at present to be just a form of 'tent-making', and is he to go all out to initiate the kinds of things he wants to do in the evenings and at weekends? Or has he reached that point to which God does bring some people, when the only way forward is to give up his full-time paid job, even if only for a time, in order to make time and space in his life for that creative venture and initiative to which he feels God is calling him? Those are the sort of questions that now face him as he faithfully follows God's leading, stage by stage.

Brian's call is to work with and on behalf of people who are impoverished in a very obvious sense. My own calling is to work with people whose inner life is impoverished and whose withholding of their treasure is an impoverishment to society – a less obvious form of impoverishment perhaps, but none the less real. I began in the last chapter to say a little about how I began to be aware of God's nudgings. Another strand in that story is that in my parish work I very gradually over a period of ten or fifteen years began to discover that I have a gift for helping adults to learn. One of the ways in which an Anglican parish priest is called upon to teach is in confirmation classes. I used to enjoy these and gradually found the courage to lay aside other people's schemes and devise my own. They seemed to be effective and people enjoyed these sessions. This approach began to spread to other areas of our parish life. We organised events in church and weekends away using similar methods. For myself this side of the work began to assume a growing importance. It came to the point where I felt that I was being nudged to move on from parish work. But I was very unclear what kind of job that would be.

When I came back from my visit to America in 1978 only one step was clear, that I would run a twelve-session course on weekday evenings. It would be designed to help people to link prayer and action in their lives and in particular to work with the notion of personal calling. I would call it Journey Inward, Journey Outward, from a book of the same name by Elizabeth O'Connor which had given me much encouragement and enlightenment in the early 1970s. It would take place in the Chapter House of St Peter's Church, Monkwearmouth. That was for me an important piece of symbolism. The church was founded in AD 674, one of the ancient holy places of the north-east of England, and is in the centre of Sunderland, an industrial town overshadowed by huge shipyard cranes. But I could see no further than putting on that course. I badly wanted to see further, but beyond that I could see absolutely nothing. For the time being I had to be content with that and obedient to that clear step that seemed to be indicated, hoping that afterwards further steps would become apparent.

Lest the examples I have given lead to too narrow an impression of the kind of things God calls people to, here briefly are three more examples originating from people in widely different circumstances.

1. Bernard works for a multi-national company making industrial equipment. The factory where he works is in an unemployment blackspot. He is responsible for hiring people for the company. He is a Christian who is thoughtful about the implications of what he does at work. He has persuaded the company that when they have to choose between people of similar qualifications and experience they will exercise a preferential choice for candidates who are unemployed.

2. 'On a foul summer day in 1985, some members of Penwith Deanery Youth Church were grumbling away when one of them had a crazy thought. "I bet there are thousands of kids", he said, "who would love to be in Cornwall even in the rain." And that's how it all began – first as a very local venture, and then, when the snowball grew too big for the Youth Church to handle by itself, as a Penwith deanery scheme: the City Kids Holiday Project. The idea was simplicity itself: to bring to West Cornwall in summer 1986 a party of children who had never had a holiday, spreading them in ones and twos among volunteer families for a week.' (Maurice Smelt, *Church Times*, 2 January 1987)

   The children came from Birmingham in the first year. They hope the idea will spread, 'linking seaside to urban wilderness'.

3. Two Quaker women living in retirement at Crawley wanted to do something for world peace. You might think that there would not be a lot that people in their position and at their time of life could do. They decided to pool their life savings and paid for a group of mothers to go on visits to Moscow and Washington, a group who came to be called Mothers for Peace.

Let no one say 'there is nothing I can do'. All that is required is some awareness of people's needs, a little imagination, some generosity, and a willingness to stick your neck out, plus an unwillingness to be put off by the impossibility of the task.

As you begin to conceive what you would love to do and take active steps towards it, you may begin to use the language of conception and birth. You may even begin to think of your infant project as your baby. That is the language of the Christian dogma of the Virgin Birth, the significance of which is widely misunderstood. Think of it as a kind of parable of the experience I am trying to describe. M. C. Richards, the American potter and poet, writes: 'We are all Mary, Virgin and undelivered, to whom the announcement has been made, in whom the infant grows!' Mary, the mother of Jesus, stands for all of us, not only women but men as well. There are times when the Lord says to you: 'The Holy Spirit will come upon you, and the power of the most high will overshadow you . . . You shall conceive and bear a son' (Luke 1:35, 31). Does that sound a bit of an exaggeration, that God says to each one of us 'you shall conceive and bear a child'? It is not of course a physical conception of a flesh and blood baby. If that were so no *man* could be responsive to God – only women. It is, if you like, a metaphor. After all it is used in everyday speech. You may say to someone who has a particular concern for a piece of work or for some undertaking, 'that's your baby'. But it is not just a figure of speech, not just a picturesque way of speaking. It goes deeper than that. The notion that what each of us has to give to the world is a child or a baby is very deep-seated. For example it is quite common in dreams. In one of his books, Christopher Bryant recounts a nightmare he once had about throwing some children off the back of a lorry and killing them. Reflecting on the dream he realised that there were the same number of children murdered in the dream as of some retreat sermons he was giving, to which he had not devoted enough preparation time. In other words the dream was saying to him: 'you have murdered those retreat addresses, your children'.

A friend has for some years had a shrewd idea of what her God-given task is to be. But she has to work full-time to support her family. It is not clear how it would be possible for her to start on it. She dreamed one night that she had had a baby, but it was getting smaller and she was very worried about it – a clear parable of the fact that with her present responsibilities she has not the time to devote to the task God is calling her to. Another dream was that she had had twins and would not be able to look after them both. This was after changing her job and it seemed to say that she could not do the job *and* the task that was beckoning her. Annunciations, callings of God, do not make for an easy life. Nor did it make life easy for Mary the mother of Jesus. But we perish inwardly if we do not eventually respond. The calling of God is what gives meaning to our own life as well as life to the world. But it can involve some difficult and painful and risky decisions.

So if we are open to the fertilising power of God, each of us has a baby that is ours to conceive, to care for and nurture: some task that is ours to do, some gift to give to the life of the world, whether it is an aspect of our job, or some voluntary work, or some leisure activity which enriches others. It may not be anything grand. It may not be a lifelong task. Christopher Bryant's children in the instance I mentioned were retreat addresses, prepared in a few short hours and delivered in a few minutes. There is nothing standard about the child or the children you are to bring forth. The only standard thing you can say about it is that in some way it is a giving of your innermost self, a giving of the gift that is particularly and peculiarly yours.

But though it is yours, though you conceive it and bring it to birth, it is not your own property any more than a flesh and blood child is. That surely is the meaning of that enigmatic but powerful story in Genesis 22 about Abraham setting out to sacrifice his son Isaac. Each of us has to be willing, sooner or later, to sacrifice – that is, to give up personal claims upon – our baby. Otherwise we become over-identified with it. It becomes for us an extension of our personality and it can become a kind of personal ego trip so that our own self-esteem comes to depend on the success of our undertaking. Often something will happen that reminds us that the child is not our exclusive possession and it may happen quite early on as a kind of salutary reminder, as with Abraham and Isaac – a reminder that our baby is conceived and born solely by the power of God and at his creative initiative. It is s/he who calls the child into being. If you like, each child of ours, in this figurative sense in which I have been speaking, is a Christ child, *God's* gift to the world through us, even though in giving it we give the essence of ourselves.

As with Mary, sooner or later our child will be the cause of pain and grief to us. That is the meaning of the legend of St Christopher. He hears the child calling in the night and cannot find him at first. That is a parable of the difficulty of discerning God's call to you, the difficulty of understanding what your task is. Then he finds the child and sets off to carry him across the river, and is nearly swept away by the force of the current and the weight of his tiny charge. That whole legend is a very powerful parable: of the difficulty of finding the child; of the risks involved in being responsive to God; of the difficulty of being single-minded enough to maintain your course without being swept away by other people's opinions or criticisms and the inevitable difficulties; and of course the joy and fulfilment in doing what you are made for.

So the dynamic of the Christian life is that we are to open ourselves ever more deeply to allowing the love of God to penetrate to our very centre. And within that centre, that place within us, from which comes all our energy and enthusiasm, we conceive the child, the task that is our creative contribution to the life of the world.

The imagery is sexual, of being loved and fertilised by God, of conceiving and bringing to birth. That is why the Virgin Birth is so central to our faith, because of its spiritual meaning. But the action that is the result of that conception is not just some inner event in the soul. The tasks we are

You shall conceive and bear a child

called to are very much in the outer world, to do with enriching the impoverished, giving sight to the blind, release to the shut in, freedom and self-determination to the oppressed. The child that you are to bring to birth will be something you do that frees or enriches or empowers others. For that is what Christ came to do, and what he comes to do again and again through each of us.

It may be that having read so far you feel a bit intimidated by all this talk about the calling of God, as though it would be to some definite and noticeable piece of work in one bound, as it were. In practice I do not think it works like that. Your response to God's calling is something that unfolds much more gradually than that, perhaps over months and years. At first it will tend to appear in miniature, so to speak, in the tiny details of daily life: for example, in the brief moment it takes to decide whether to be honest or not at a particular point in a conversation that seems to call for it; or whether you take refuge in silence or in pleasantries. You might notice it in becoming aware of a small kindness you could do for someone: and you go ahead – or you hold back, afraid that you will look foolish, or that your offer will be rejected, or that it will be misunderstood.

These are the kinds of ways you begin to be aware of God's personal calling; not usually in an invitation to take some big step, but in these tiny daily opportunities to be truer to what you are or could be. Over time, a new mindset may begin to be established in you. As you begin to live a bit more in this kind of way, you may sense yourself invited to take more distinct and more noticeable initiatives that begin to look to yourself and others more like a calling from God. But, writ large or small, the process is the same, a willingness to offer something, and risk criticism, or ridicule, or rejection.

TWO EXERCISES

1. If you were to take a step, however small, towards your dream conceived in Chapter 12, what would it be? Reflect on this over the next few days. Take it to God in prayer. Have a conversation with Jesus about it in your journal.

When a course of action is beginning to become clear, and when you feel ready, talk it over with one or two godly and perceptive people. If you have been sharing the fruits of these exercises with a small group, talk it over with them. Ideally spiritual guides should have three qualities – wisdom about God and the way s/he works, an understanding of our inner life as human beings, and an awareness of the public, political and institutional aspect of our life. If you can find someone who combines all three you are indeed fortunate! However, it may be possible to find several people who between them have something of these three qualities. Get their reactions to your proposed course of action. Their opinions will give you helpful feedback: but of course you will have to take the responsibility yourself for any step you decide to take in the end.

2. One of the classic examples of personal calling in the Bible is that of Moses. Take time to ponder on the following verses from Exodus, and write in your journal your reactions to the questions alongside them. Just jot down what comes to your mind as you reflect on them, no matter how apparently inconsistent or even 'unrealistic' it may seem to you at present. Notice what comes to your mind. For the moment, leave aside the question whether it is the time to be acting on any of it.

Moses	**You**
Brought up in Pharaoh's palace (Exodus 2:10)	What Pharaohs (oppressors or oppressive ideas) are you aware of – in society? where you live? where you work? within yourself? . . . .
Goes to be with his own people and sees their hard labour (Exodus 2:11)	As you look round your locality, the places where you live and work, or the wider world, who are the people whose condition particularly touches your heart? Don't just think of the people you feel you ought to be concerned about. Who are the people

whose needs actually touch your heart most? .... On whose behalf do you feel angry? ....

Rushes into action without a call and kills the Egyptian (Exodus 2:12)	What jobs or tasks have you taken on 'uncalled' e.g. simply out of a sense of 'ought'? ....

There's nothing necessarily wrong with that. Each of us needs to do our share of those. The important question for you here is:- have you taken on too many tasks that feel like that to you? .... Have you taken on a particular task or tasks that you know in your heart you shouldn't have? Just be aware of this – it may not be the right time to act upon your awareness . . .

Runs for his life and goes and sits by a well in Midian (Exodus 2:15)	What 'being' time do you have in your life? ....

What time for doing nothing in particular? ....
Are you aware that there have been 'fallow' times in your life? ....
Is it in some way a fallow time for you at present?
Does it need to be? ....

Stands around tending the sheep. Sees a bush burning and goes to have a look (Exodus 3:1–3)	In your 'being' time, whatever form that takes – or if it's fallow time for you at present – do you open your awareness to people, to the world, to nature? ....

Or do you cocoon yourself? . . .
Do you perhaps need to cocoon yourself in some way, or for some reason? . . . .

Becomes aware of God's call to him to bring the Israelites out of Egypt (Exodus 3:7–10)

The prayers and pleadings of all kinds of people in all sorts of situations are poured out towards God every moment of the day. When you think of the people whose condition particularly touches your heart, reflect on what it might mean for you to hear their prayer. . . .

Is there something you long to do?
Is there something you long to see happen, but wish someone else would do it? . . . .

Feels inadequate to the task. 'Who am I that I should go to Pharaoh and bring the Israelites out of Egypt?' (Exodus 3:11) 'O Lord, I have never been eloquent, neither in the past nor since you have spoken to your servant. I am slow of speech and tongue.' Then the Lord said to him, 'Who gives speech to mortals? Who makes them mute or deaf, seeing or blind? Is it not I, the Lord? Now go, and I will be with your mouth and teach you what you are to speak.' But he said, 'O my Lord, please send someone else' (Exodus 4:10–13)

Do you feel inadequate to do anything about it yourself?
In what specific way or ways do you feel inadequate? . . . .

WHO CARES?

I thought I saw a dark and stormy ocean. Over it the black clouds hung heavily, through which every now and then loud thunders rolled, and vivid lightnings flashed; and the winds moaned, and the waves rose and foamed and fretted and broke.... In that ocean I thought I saw myriads of poor human beings plunging and floating and shouting and shrieking and cursing and struggling and drowning.... And out of this dark angry ocean I saw a mighty rock rise up above the black clouds that overhung the stormy sea; and all around the base of this rock I saw a vast platform; and up onto this platform I saw with delight a number of the poor, struggling, drowning wretches continually climbing out of the angry ocean; and I saw that a number of those who were already safe on the platform helped these to reach the same place of safety....

And as I looked I saw that the occupants of that platform were quite a mixed company. That is, they divided themselves into different sets, and were employed in quite different ways; but there were only a very few, comparatively, who seemed to make it their business to get the people out of the sea.... Some were absorbed night and day in trading in order to make gain and store up their savings in boxes and by other means. Many spent their time in amusing themselves with growing flowers on the side of the rock; others in painting pieces of cloth, or in performing music, or in dressing themselves up in different ways and walking about to be admired. Some occupied themselves very much in eating and drinking, and others were greatly taken up with arguing about the poor drowning creatures in the sea, and what would become of them, or in going through rounds of curious religious ceremonies....

And all this time the struggling, shrieking multitudes were floating about in the dark sea, quite nearby – quite near enough to have been pulled out.
(from Letter 28, 'Who cares?', of *The General's Letters, 1885*, by William Booth)

14

Feeling Inadequate

There are many examples of the calling of God in the Bible, and more often than not the recipients of the call are fearful and afraid to respond. Samuel was afraid to tell Eli, his master, about the rather dire message he had received from God in the night (1 Sam. 3:15). Ananias was given by God a message to give to Saul of Tarsus (Acts 9). He hesitated, with some justification, in view of Saul's reputation for violence towards Christians. Jonah, when he heard the call of God to go to Nineveh, immediately booked a passage on a ship going in the opposite direction. (The little book of Jonah, incidentally, is a lovely parable about evading and resisting the calling of God.)

We also read frequently of the feelings of inadequacy evoked by the calling of God. God tells Gideon, 'Go in this might of yours and deliver Israel from the hand of Midian; I hereby commission you'. 'But sir, how can I deliver Israel?' Gideon remonstrates, 'My clan is the weakest in Manasseh and I am the least in my family' (Judg. 6:14).

Jeremiah's response to God's call is, 'Ah, Lord God! I do not know how to speak. I am only a child'. Isaiah feels he is not good enough, 'I am a man of unclean lips and I live among a people of unclean lips' (Isa. 6:5). Elijah does his absolute best for God, and is actually rather effective. So much so, that Jezebel has it in for him, and Elijah has to flee to the desert for safety. He asks to die, 'It is enough;

now, O Lord, take away my life, for I am no better than my forebears' (1 Kings 19:4). And then there is the famous example of David, not so much to do with subjective feelings of inadequacy, but with someone else's estimation of it (1 Sam. 16). Samuel had been told by God to anoint one of the sons of Jesse as king. Jesse offers each of his sons in turn for inspection – some quite impressive people. Having seen all of them, Samuel says that God has not chosen any of them. It then transpires that Jesse had not even bothered to call David, the youngest, a mere country bumpkin.

You may have some favourites among these, or perhaps another one not mentioned here. One that I find myself drawn to again and again is Moses. He is such a marvellous mixture of human compassion, enthusiasm and inadequacy, and the power of God somehow to make such amazing use of all that when it is given willingly and freely. The account in Exodus 2 begins with his birth, his abandonment in the rush basket and his rescue by Pharaoh's daughter. It all sounds very improbable and full of coincidence. But no more so than God's call of you or me from the womb and through all the vicissitudes of our young life. You may put a lot of it down to chance, perhaps even to mischance. But as you grow older you may begin to see the mysterious hand of God in it all, every bit as sure as it was with Moses.

As we saw in the exercise at the end of the last chapter, Moses is full of feelings of not being up to what God is calling him to do. He is quite right. His hesitancy is well-founded. He does not have what it takes and he knows it. To which the answer from God is, 'I am with you.' This is an authentic mark of calling. God's call is *always* to tasks beyond our powers. If at any time you think otherwise I suspect that either it is not God who is calling or you are overestimating your powers. Moses was acutely aware of his shortcomings and of his basic lack of the necessary gifts: 'Oh Lord, I am no great speaker, I simply haven't got what it takes.' God promises to be with him and to tell him what to say, but Moses pleads, 'Please send someone else instead of me.' Eventually God agrees to give him

Aaron to help him and do the public speaking. The whole thing is a beautifully accurate parable of the process of being given a call and some of the feelings that go with it. We then read on (e.g. up to Chapter 20 of Exodus, and from Chapter 11 of Numbers) about all the problems, of how people let him down, of how things went wrong and he got blamed, of how at times he felt like throwing in the towel; but we also hear of the hope and even of the joy of the journey and of God's unfailing faithfulness.

When Brian began to be aware of the call to work with and on behalf of the poor in a council housing estate those were some of the thoughts jostling for attention in his mind. He drew them in a circle, chasing one another round and round.

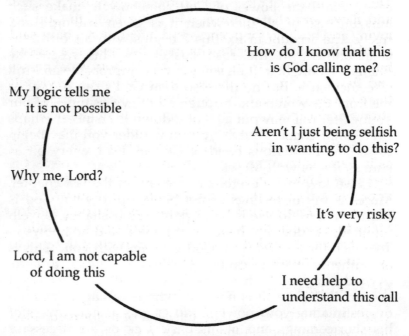

How do I know that this is God calling me?

My logic tells me it is not possible

Aren't I just being selfish in wanting to do this?

Why me, Lord?

It's very risky

Lord, I am not capable of doing this

I need help to understand this call

These feelings of inadequacy are not just feelings of low self-esteem. They are objectively justified. We need to learn to trust in God's power, the power that is beyond us in every sense and which takes what we offer of ourselves and uses it for the mysterious work of furthering his kingdom.

I remember hearing a sermon once by Gordon Cosby, the minister of the Church of the Saviour in Washington, DC. He used the parable of the Good Samaritan to illustrate two 'humps' that we have to get over in the matter of calling. When you first hear the parable it is natural to identify with the Samaritan: in fact we are invited to do so, to think of ourselves as potential helpers, good and strong people who will do all kinds of useful and constructive things. The first hump to get over is to realise that we are not all that good, and not all that strong. Sooner or later as we hit our limitations and ineffectiveness we realise that we have much in common with the man in the ditch. That is an important step, to become aware of our wounds and flaws and shortcomings and bring them to God for loving and healing, forgiveness and integration. I have said a little about that in earlier chapters. But there is a second hump to negotiate, to realise that *with* all our weaknesses and flaws we are nevertheless called to active service. If there is a temptation to begin with to think of ourselves as strong and capable, there is a similar temptation as we become aware of our weakness and woundedness, to feel we are disqualified by it and to hang around the hospital, as it were, as though on permanent sick leave. The fact is that when enough healing and integrative work has been done we are called to action. We are not required to be perfect specimens of humanity to be used in God's service. Many times we find it is at the very point of our woundedness that we are called to serve. The important thing is to get our dependence over on to God.

AN EXERCISE

Read Matthew 14:22–33. Use this as a basis for meditation in the way described in the exercise in Chapter 7.

Be in the boat yourself and hear Jesus' invitation addressed to you. How do you respond? What happens? What does he do? How do you feel?

If you like, *after* you have done the meditation, write a letter to yourself. Imagine you are writing from your deathbed to yourself at your present age. The subject of your letter is the course of action you are contemplating. What do you want to say to yourself in your letter?

THE TIME FOR FIGS

There twinges in my heart
  a pity for that fig tree – barren –
  Caught up within the eyes of Christ,
  Cursed by his lips.

There echo in my soul
  Defences for the tree's unburdened limbs
  Held light against the sky –
Perhaps
  because it's I
  who *am* the fig tree
    content to wait the seasons out.

But *now* is the time for figs –
  Season or not –
  I've looked for the sun too long.
  Yearned for the rain to come and comfort me.
  The earth to gather and to nourish.

It is the time for figs –
  The hungry and the weak pass by
  And the blossoms are an empty, bitter food.

It is the time for bearing.
  Oh Jesus, look again on me
  And cause in me such heaviness of fruit
  That it shall fall unreached for round your foot.

The season is ripe:
  It is the time for figs.
                    Ann Maureen Gallagher IHM

15

Get into Action

This book offers an outline of what I see as a many-sided process. Each chapter describes an aspect of it. Some of them may have spoken to your condition more than others, depending on 'where you are', if I may use the phrase metaphorically. Coming now to this one you may feel that your next step is not clear, or that now is not the time for action. That must be for you to judge. If the next step is not clear there may be more work to do on some of the other aspects of the search. It will come clear eventually if you are sincere and whole-hearted in your search. Martin Buber says somewhere that when you finally get round to asking 'What have I to do?' with an open willingness to hear, the answer that comes back is: 'You shall not withhold yourself.'

That, sooner or later, is the key – a generous willingness to live the answer, rather than theorising about it. There comes a time when you will get no more clarity about a call until you have taken whatever practical next step has become clear, however small it may seem. A fairly reliable sign of such a step being right is that you feel content about it in your quieter moments. It is not something you are bouncing yourself into, and it is not just some scheme worked out on rational lines alone. If you have done your inner work as far as you can, the next move is to take that step.

It will always be to some degree a step of faith. It may consist of writing a letter or organising a public meeting. It may be having a word with your boss at work or putting a case to your next board meeting. It may be offering to do the flowers at your church or resigning your paid employment to go and live with the homeless. However small or large a step it is, you will be setting out on what is for you an unknown and untried path. The path of faith is a fine line between naivety and hard-headed realism. You do need to set out in faith, but you need also to have applied your mind to it so that you are as aware as it is possible to be of what you might be letting yourself in for. But though it is important to be aware of the risks, do not be afraid of appearing naive. Gordon Cosby says: 'The most helpful experiments are accomplished by people who are too naive to know what they are getting into. The wise and experienced know too much ever to accomplish the impossible' (Elizabeth O'Connor, *Journey Inward, Journey Outward*, p. 135). There is an old saying about the bumble-bee, that according to the laws of aerodynamics it cannot fly because its wings are too small for its weight. But the bumble-bee is ignorant of these laws and manages to fly quite well. True or not, it is an encouraging thought.

Since quite a lot of what I say is based on or coloured by my own experience, perhaps you will bear with me if I continue my story beyond the winter of 1978–9 when I ran the first Journey Inward, Journey Outward course. That course went very well, so much so that within a few months I was running another. That second one was I think the worst course I have ever run, with one possible exception. One of the problems was that there were too many uncommitted members who sat somewhat light to the assignments which I gave between sessions. But I felt that it was my fault that it went awry and I felt really hammered. I learned more from it, though, than from any other I have done. In particular it made me realise that the course that I offer is not basically a group process. The people who came who expected the group somehow to do it for them, to be carried along by the group, got little from it. It became much clearer to me that what I offer is basically an individual process, a journey that an individual can only make for herself. I now say to people it is the exercises which are the backbone of the course. The weekly sessions are mainly for sharing how you get on with the exercises. Ever since then I have run the course on that assumption and it has formed my whole approach in these pages. So I learned much from that course, much more than any of the participants did!

In the following months I ran several similar courses as a sideline while vicar of a parish. Meanwhile I was looking for another job which would allow me to develop this work further. Over about two years I applied for seven or eight jobs and was turned down for all of them. At the time it was quite painful, though the discipline of writing each job application helped me each time to articulate a little more clearly what I wanted to do. But there was another side to it, much more hidden, which only surfaced from time to time. For example, one of the jobs I applied for, and was within an ace of getting, was in the south of England. The night before I went for interview I dreamed that I was trying to kill a Purple Emperor, a rare species of butterfly. I did not succeed and it survived, somewhat mutilated. The following morning I told my wife the dream as we were driving to the station, and I said to her that in an odd way I felt that going for a job down south, which would mean leaving the north-east, was a kind of betrayal; and the dream had drawn my attention to that. With hindsight it is much clearer that I was to stay in the north-east, and I am now so thankful that I did not get any of those jobs. But at the time it was much more difficult to discern what God was up to and what he wanted. I still had the 'dream' from 1975 – about 'an Iona in the north-east' – but I was not at all clear what its implications were for me, apart from running the Journey Inward, Journey Outward courses from time to time. For most of that two-year period I had the last verse of Psalm 27 pinned up over my desk: 'O wait for the Lord, stand firm and he will strengthen your heart: and wait I say for the Lord.' Latterly I added some words of St Paul: 'Faithful is he who calls you.' I devoutly hoped he was!

In the spring of 1981, after being turned down for yet another job, I began to toy with the idea of setting something up off my own bat. I decided to talk with two other clergy, old friends of mine with similar interests. At the back of my mind was the idea that we might form some kind of joint enterprise. I invited them over for a morning. All I said to them was that I felt we should wait on God. Imagine my astonishment when towards the end of our discussion one of them said, 'Have you ever thought of simply resigning your parish and setting up a trust to employ you? I have been thinking for some time that it might be a way forward.' I hardly registered what he said at the time. But as I thought about it afterwards my heart began to dance. What a marvellous idea! Such a bold idea had not occurred to me; I would not have expected people to have that much confidence in me to support me in that way. But now someone had suggested it, I was for a day or two walking on air. Ironically enough the person who suggested it was someone who had attended that disastrous course I mentioned earlier. So it felt like a vote of confidence. The following Friday I saw him at a meeting. Afterwards I told him how enthusiastic I felt. 'Oh,' he said, waving a hand dismissively, 'don't rush into anything. It was only an idea.' I felt utterly deflated and quite depressed as I drove home. But the seed had been sown.

When I feel more than usually chewed up about something I usually ring some friend who I know will listen. As soon as I got home I did just that and arranged a session for the following morning. In the course of an hour's conversation that Saturday morning in May 1981 I decided that I would resign my parish and set up a trust as my friend had suggested. If the other two were not ready for such a step, I was quite clear that I was. I came home and Elizabeth and I talked it over for most of the rest of the day. She was actually quite pleased about the prospect. She had never been keen on the vicar's wife role. It would be a release for her as well. But there were two enormous questions to face. We had three school-age children. My wife had no qualification which would enable her to bring in much of an income. How on earth would we support ourselves? We would have to move out of the vicarage as soon as my resignation took effect: where could we live? But we decided to give it a try. We would aim to leave at the end of the year. That gave us seven months to find answers to those two questions. Meanwhile I rang and cancelled a job enquiry I had begun to make, as a symbol of our decision not to look for ready-made niches any more. I was going to have to carve one out for myself.

During the next few days, though I felt basically settled about the decision, I had periods of feeling quite low. I found that I felt better when I began to write down what I wanted to do. It was almost as though even the tiniest step towards the target got my energy and enthusiasm flowing; whereas when I neglected it for too long I left myself open to feeling low again.

I began to reflect about the possibility of some ecumenical association of Christians in the north-east who would live out their calling and have some common discipline to enable and encourage them in it. I began to jot down the kind of instruction and preparation that would be necessary. After a few days I had articulated my own sense of calling in the following way:

1. I want to work towards forming an ecumenical company of Christians who are committed to both the inward and outward journey and to disciplines to enable this.
2. I want, further, to work towards forming groups of 'called' people round tasks in society or church, so that Christians can be effective ministers of the gospel.
3. This company of Christians needs to have some public manifestation in the Tyne-Wear conurbation so that it can be seen and related to by the unchurched. There needs to be some way others can be in touch with our life without being committed.
4. My further hope is that this company of people would

be connected in some way with one of the holy places of the north-east, to draw also on the spiritual capital of the past.

5. I believe I shall never give myself a chance to do this unless I leave the parish ministry and exercise this new kind of priesthood wholeheartedly. This means looking for some way of being paid and supporting the family.

Meanwhile I made arrangements to talk with several godly persons just to check out whether they thought I was round the twist. The first, a good friend, came to our house to talk. I think he thought I was! I told him more or less what I have written in the last paragraph. He did not react much to the content, but made some very helpful suggestions about the practical side. As we were talking the doorbell rang. While I went to answer it he at once took Elizabeth by the arm and asked: 'Are you all right?' as though she were in some grave danger.

One of the people I asked to see was Brother Jonathan at the Friary at Alnmouth, whom I knew slightly. He said: 'Well, it could be of God. It's crazy enough.' But he pointed out that the touchstone would be whether the two practical problems, a house and an income, could be solved.

The house question raised itself rather more immediately than we expected. Almost by chance we found a suitable one for which the vendors wanted nearly £27,000, an unimaginable sum for us. We slept on it and prayed on it and decided to offer the asking price, wondering where on earth the money would come from. I went and talked to everyone I could think of who might have money and drew a complete blank. About three weeks later on my day off when the children had just come home from school and I had my feet up, the vicarage doorbell rang. I went to answer it and there on the doorstep was a friend, an ex-parishioner, looking a bit long-faced. I invited him into the study and, with an inward sigh, resigned myself to listening for the next hour to whatever his troubles might be. He sat down on the edge of the armchair. 'My wife and I have heard about your proposed step,' he began, 'and we have prayed about it and we would like to put £2,000 at your disposal.' I nearly fell off my chair!

In the next few months, one way or another, seven others followed and offered interest-free loans of various sizes. Our solicitor drew up a deed of common ownership with Elizabeth and me and each of the others owning stated percentages of the value of the house. This support not only made the move possible; it has been a tremendous encouragement and endorsement of the work.

The other question was where our income would come from. One possible source I had tried was John Habgood, then Bishop of Durham. Over the previous three or four years I had met him occasionally to talk about how my thinking was developing and he had been very supportive. But I had tried without success to persuade him to create a post in the diocese that would enable me to develop my work. I knew he favoured sabbaticals – time off on full pay for study or writing or further training. I had at that time been ordained twenty-one years. I decided I would ask him if he would agree to pay me a vicar's salary for six months for every seven years I had served since my ordination. In effect I was asking him to pay me on a sabbatical basis from the end of December 1981, when we planned to leave the parish, until the end of June 1983.

I was due to see him on 22 June 1981 to put this suggestion to him. I was full of apprehension. On the previous Wednesday I wrote in my journal: 'Lord, I am worried about what happens if the bishop refuses on Monday. *Please* may we have his support to launch out.' God: 'You have my support; what more do you need?' Me: 'Yes, but we need financial help to get started.' God: 'You'll get it.' Me: 'Thank you, Lord. I know we shall, help my unbelief.' Since making the decision on that Saturday in May, in my heart of hearts I was as sure as I could be that it was the right course of action. But many times my confidence wobbled about how it could be done. And of course, concurrently, I was looking at other possible ways of doing it.

On the Monday I went to see the bishop, and at that stage was able to say we had been promised 50 per cent of the cash support we needed for a house. I hoped that would indicate that we already had substantial backing. I put my request to him. 'That is one of the easier things you have asked me,' he replied, and more or less gave me an off-the-cuff undertaking, though he said he would confirm it officially the following week. Once again I was walking on air. In the car driving home it suddenly struck me: 'Help! He's agreed!' I began to realise, 'What a privilege, what a responsibility! To start something from scratch, with full responsibility for what happens – no one to tell me how to do it, no one to pat me on the back, no one to blame if it goes wrong. Very alarming, but a marvellous challenge and opportunity.' It meant that I could get started and had eighteen months in which to set up a trust and get some financial backing. Meanwhile Elizabeth had got on to a course at Sunderland Poly leading to a certificate of qualification for social work. If she got through, and if the project was slow to grow financially, she could start earning nine days after the bishop's money ran out. The likelihood of us ending up on state benefits began to recede very considerably.

There were many ups and downs, joys and crises between then and the end of 1981 when I left the parish; but there was no doubt in my mind that it was the right step to take. The same could not be said of what happened next.

After a week or two of settling in, the first thing I did was to go to Lindisfarne on 18 January 1982 to join in the eight-day vigil which used to be held at Marygate House each year, a mixture of retreat and prayer and discussion on issues of the day. I felt I needed time to reflect and pray about how on earth I was going to set about the task. It was a fairly relaxed time, and most evenings the half dozen people who were there would repair to the local pub on the main street of the village. We would sit round the open fire and talk about this and that. One evening we heard that the pub was up for sale. We each looked at one another, wondering if the others were thinking the same. I think I may have been the one to say it out loud, and even as

I did so I wondered if I were just being mischievous: 'How about buying it?' Marygate is fairly short of bedroom accommodation and the pub had eight simple guest rooms upstairs; plus we could still run the bar as an open opportunity to make low-key contact with holiday-makers who visit the island in summer, as well as with the islanders who might otherwise easily be alienated by the opening of a conference house. As we talked one of our number was already thinking he would be glad to work there as the barman.

Over the next few days we talked more about it among ourselves and with one or two others. I began to feel very torn about the whole thing. I felt I could only join in wholeheartedly if we were working towards an umbrella trust that would sponsor me and pay me. If such an umbrella organisation developed in time, I would have no need to make my own arrangements with the Charity Commissioners. But I would need to be sure that any trustees who were appointed knew and understood what my project was about. Otherwise my newborn infant could get pushed around quite a bit, and might not survive.

We met regularly over the next six months, until a meeting in the July which finally made me realise that our plans and hopes at this stage did not involve the same risk for them as they did for me. None of them had yet crossed any Rubicons. I also realised that six out of my eighteen months had already gone by and not one pound had been raised towards employing me. Mercifully I was baled out at this point by the trustees of Marygate House, who had been in existence since 1970. They generously offered to adopt my project, which easily fitted under the terms of their trust deed. They have never been in a position to support it financially, but this link saved me from having to set up a trust of my own. It also gave me a lovely low-key link with the island, which is one of the main holy places of the north-east.

My part in the pub episode was not a creditable one – not because it was a bad idea in itself; on the contrary it had tremendous potential – but because *for me* it was a seduction. It was a temptation to join with others and feel less alone. It was less than three weeks since I had set out, feeling very unclear how to proceed and needing time and care to let the thing grow in its own way like a tree according to the inner laws of its own growth. And here was I risking this tiny seedling, exposing it to the boots and spades of other gardeners before it even had any leaves or distinguishing marks. As a matter of fact one of the things I found very difficult to communicate to the others was exactly what it was I did hope for. I felt very much that their understanding of what I was trying to articulate was coloured by their own hopes: and I had absolutely nothing concrete to show them, only words. This is a period of very great danger for any called person, when their project is little more than a gleam in their eye. Not only is their project very vulnerable at this stage, but they too are very exposed to temptation, to being diverted from their calling. It is no accident that Jesus' temptations came right at the beginning of his ministry.

I have told this little bit of my own story because it gives me some pegs on which to hang a few points about the business of getting into action. But let me make it quite clear that I am in no way wanting to suggest 'this is the way to get into action' or 'this is the kind of action to get into'. The way is different for each of us. And the action is different too. With that proviso, I hope it will do as a way of introducing six general points which you can translate into your own situation and reflect about in connection with whatever step you are considering.

First *be willing to take responsibility yourself for your action*, however modest a step it is. I have already begun to illustrate the importance of this in the last paragraph but one. Perhaps an even clearer example is provided by my inviting my two friends to talk about the possibility of some kind of joint enterprise. I suppose I was hoping in a vague way that some joint course of action would emerge. When it became apparent that that was not how they saw it, I almost felt that it put a cross rather than a tick against the possibility of my launching out. In other words I had handed over to them some of the responsibility for my own life and my response to God: that is why I felt depressed after my brief encounter on that Friday. In the conversation with that other friend on the Saturday morning, I in effect took back that responsibility on to my own shoulders.

Let me put it another way. It is one thing to say: 'Let's meet to see what we can do about encouraging co-oper-ation here in this town.' It is quite another to say: 'I am starting a conciliation service for neighbour disputes on this estate: are you interested in joining me?' In the first example no one is making any commitments: and what is actually going to be done is left open. People may have very different ideas of what ought to be done, and each will want to pull things their own way. This is a recipe for a talk shop, if you are not careful. In the second it is quite clear that *you* are going to do something and are not going to hang about waiting to see what others will do: this means that others have much much more idea what they will be letting themselves in for if they join you: and it is easier for them to decide whether to or not. It means that both you and they are free agents. You are not secretly hoping the others' decisions will carry you along. This is a recipe for action.

To put it yet another way, there are three major steps in life that no one can take for you – being born, responding to God's personal call, and dying: and they all have some-thing in common with one another. This may sound very individualist. In one sense it is. But if by that you mean to convey that it is isolationist, I shall totally disagree with you. I believe that potentially the most genuine kinds of community are promoted where the people concerned are all exercising their particular gift. Sometimes what passes for community is a group of people huddling together for fear of taking responsibility for their own lives.

Secondly *do not expect signs from heaven to decide your course of action*. That is another way of abdicating responsi-bility, in this case the responsibility of working at the issue of calling in your own life. Someone was applying for a new job and had been offered it. She was not sure whether it was God's will that she should take it. So she told a friend: 'If it's cloudy next Monday morning, I'll take it: if not, I won't.' It was, and she did. That is a rather extreme example of a not uncommon attitude, which looks for outer signs as a substitute for inner work. It is not that signs are not relevant: it is that the inner work needs to be done as thoroughly as a person is able. Any 'signs' may then confirm the decision already taken. So, for example, if I had been looking for signs in this sense, my experience of the second Journey Inward, Journey Outward course might have put me off for good. I might have read the message as, 'Give up, you're no good at it!' I certainly had a lot to learn, but the experience did not make me radically doubt what I was to be about.

It comes down to the need for *enough* clarity about your call as you take each step along the way. You will probably not see far ahead. All it needs is clarity about the *next* step. That then gives you the inner basis for coping with all the inevitable difficulties and problems that will arise. Suppose a group of people want to buy a house as a home of healing; they are on the point of doing so, but they encounter some practical difficulties. One of them says: 'If the house is put back on the market, we must assume that the project was never God's will in the first place.' In such a case I would suspect that too much of the sense of calling has been associated with the house, what you might call 'the magic of the place', and not enough with the people. They are somehow expecting the building to do it for them. The call needs to be articulated by *each* of the people involved as clearly as possible. Then, when you get to the point of knowing in your hearts that the next step is to acquire a property, the inevitable difficulties will not make you doubt your call. As someone said, 'You will go round them, over them, under them, or through them', in your joyful knowledge that this is the task that is yours to do. If you need a property as the next step and there are insuperable difficulties about that one, go out and look for another one that will provide what you need.

Thirdly *articulate your call*. In the first place do this for yourself. Write down as clearly as you can what you hope for in the long term and what your next step is. For me, having to make a number of job applications over a two-year period helped towards this. It is true that with a job application you have to think out what you will offer in the context of a particular job specification: basically the terms are dictated by your prospective employer. But in practice I found that each time I wrote out a job application I became a little clearer in my own mind what I would like to offer, even if it could not be written as part of the application form for that particular job. The discipline of doing each application threw me back each time to reflect about what I would love to do if I had the opportunity. So when, after making the decision to resign the parish, I came to articulate it for myself without the limitations of any job specification, it came clear in a matter of a day or two.

Fourthly *when you feel ready, be willing to go public*, to tell people what you are going to do. This may mean coping with feeling arrogant or foolish as you do so. You will feel, as Moses did, that you simply have not got what it takes. As long as you have done your inner work enough, it is simply a matter of putting up with the feelings and not letting them get to you. And do be willing to *ask* for support, in action or in cash or in other ways. The worst that can happen is that the answer will be 'no', and you may risk looking a bit foolish. Much more often, in my very limited experience, the answers are 'yes' in wonderful and often totally unexpected ways. It is a very humbling experience to find that even if you take a tiny step in response to God's call, s/he comes nine-tenths of the way to meet you, though often not in the way you expect. Sometimes, s/he does that even when you have made a mess of it; like my experience with the pub. After all, in the end that led to my link with Marygate and Holy Island. If you are only vaguely near enough to the thread of your life you become aware that, whatever difficulties befall you, mysteriously the wind is behind you. This is all a very sobering experience. It makes you realise how totally dependent you are on God, and how incredibly generous, God is.

Fifthly *take a practical step to correspond with your inner intention*. When I made the decision to resign the parish and launch out I felt it was right to cancel the current job enquiry. Twice more in the next week or two I had occasion to say no to job approaches. But it was that first deliberate step of cancelling the enquiry that was important, otherwise it would have been tempting to keep a lot of options open 'just in case'. I am not saying that keeping options open would be inappropriate for someone else in different circumstances. But for me then cancelling the enquiry *was* the next practical step. It may not seem much, not a big step to take, but it was important for me at that time, in order to express in action my inner disposition. What all this really boils down to is that there comes a time when the thinking and talking and reflecting has to stop. You have to be willing to begin to lay yourself on the line. 'You shall not withhold yourself,' says Buber.

Sixthly *do not put the Lord your God to the test*. I sometimes hear of people doing rather foolhardy things like actually signing a contract on a property without having the money to complete the transaction, and expecting God to provide it. This is putting God to the test, unless you are prepared to face what might happen if the worst came to the worst – in this instance, not being in a position to complete, and losing several thousand pounds of deposit. It is not that God does not provide; sometimes s/he does in very wonderful and unexpected ways. It is the *assumption* that God will provide that seems to me to be wrong. In my view genuine faith is composed of *both* a deep trust in God *and* the use of all the wits and intelligence that God has given you. It is not simply a matter of shutting your eyes and jumping.

I have tried in this book to describe an approach to action which springs from within you, that is an expression of your gifts and leanings, that goes with the grain of your being, so that what you do for the kingdom in whatever sphere, however difficult and intractable, you do it because you love to do it. In *Think On These Things* Krishnamurti writes:

> don't battle against society, don't tackle dead tradition, unless you have this love in you, for your struggle will be meaningless and you will merely create more mischief. Whereas, if you deeply feel what is right and can therefore stand alone, then your action borne of love will have extraordinary significance, it will have vitality, beauty. (quoted in Elizabeth O'Connor, *Eighth Day of Creation*, p. 98)

When I look back at what I wrote in 1981 about my sense of call I realise that I have achieved virtually nothing except as regards item 5, which was only the next step in any case. Item 1 had the tiniest of beginnings in that for three years I and one other person, a community worker, formed what we grandly called the Lindisfarne Network. We used to meet fortnightly to be accountable to one another for our inward and outward journey, and once a year on Holy Island we each made a commitment to the respective tasks to which we are called. The network could hardly be said to have existed at all; and in the end my companion offered himself for ordination, which was really one in the eye for me, whose whole aim is to grow committed *lay* people! Items 2 and 3 seem further off than ever, and they always felt a long way off. So outwardly I have virtually nothing to show for the last eighteen years. I am not being self-deprecating in saying this: in view of what I hope for it is the literal truth. But meanwhile I thoroughly enjoy what I do, working with people in all kinds of ways and places on this business of personal calling. Rightly or wrongly I do not fret about my lack of success. It just takes much longer 'to grow' called people than I had ever guessed. But the longing for a network of 'called' people is undimmed, not least because I believe that 'called' people are such an encouragement to others, and not just to their immediate circle. And people need all the encouragement they can get.

So as you get into action, enjoy the process. Do not feel that your life and your self-esteem stand or fall by what you achieve. Catch a glimpse of the dream and let it draw you. Keep the longing alive in your heart. Have a whale of a time doing what you do. And let God take care of the outcome and make of it what he will.

AN EXERCISE

Take the (next) step that has become clear to you. Afterwards write in your journal about what happened and how you felt.

Or, if reading this book has been your first introduction to the kind of process I have been offering, it may be that you are not ready to get into action in the kind of way that I am suggesting. Your journey outward does need to grow from your journey inward, and that will take time. It may be that there is more inner work to be done before you are ready for that. If so, what is the next step that needs taking in your inward journey?

ON STARTING A PEACEMAKING GROUP: A PARABLE OF SOCIAL ACTION

If you are working in a serious way at creating any sort of counter-culture institution, it is so difficult and the experience is so exhausting that unless it is coming out of a growing understanding of grace, I believe you are likely to burn out . . . In peacemaking, for example, you are in for something that is a long-range movement . . . I would hope that you will not be burning out in three or four years . . .

Motivation is absolutely crucial to the way in which you go because the more magnificent and enticing and tremendous your vision, the sooner it will exhaust you unless you are coming out of this grace stance. The very fact that the vision is so immense means that you are trying to live up to it, and you are trying to carry through on what you see. But you cannot carry through, for the vision is always going to be much more immense than what you can do. You will get into it, and you will hit your own impotence. You will learn that the situation is much worse than you ever thought, and those demonic structures are more demonic than you had any idea of. You will not realize how difficult is the fulfilling of the vision and how demonic are the structures until you start tangling with them.

If you are operating out of a *grace* stance . . . then you will be enjoying yourself, you will be able to stay with it. To *block* others from coming into the group, all you need to do is to wander around with a heavy load, all you cannot do anything about, to feel impotent, and to get angry at the system . . .

I do not have any answers, but I do ask, 'what is your motivation?' Are you going to explore the possibility of getting a peacemaking group started simply because God has given you the capacity to see something which is very exciting? Because when you see it, you are called to participate, and it is a joy to do? And when you find yourself up against all the barriers that you knew were going to be there, will you still be having a great time? You may say your motivation is 55% grace and 45% obligation and demand and law for you; or it may be 10% grace and about 90% law. Simply start where you are and start moving in the direction of grace. *There are not many people who function out of grace.* (Gordon Cosby, *Handbook for World Peacemaker Groups*, 1979, pp. 10–11)

How Could the Church Help?

It is frightening the number of people I know in the Church who at some time or another have thought of offering themselves for ordination. It is frightening because it betrays the narrowness of the Church's notion of vocation. It is a sign of the narrowness that we communicate by what we *live* as a Church, that is, our common life and worship, as opposed to what we *say*. For an ordination the vast Norman cathedral at Durham is full of people to celebrate the fact that these people who are to be ordained are responding to God's call. In a way I have no quarrel with that: when anyone responds to the calling of God it is a matter for celebration. But what public, churchly celebration is there when someone responds to God's call to paint icons, say, or to run a soup kitchen for the homeless or to start a housing co-operative in an inner city area, or to dedicate their life to finding a cure for cancer? Is there celebration of any kind for this? Is there any recognition, or even suspicion, in our churches that people do those kind of things with a strong sense of God's calling? In my experience, not a lot.

If you talk of vocation, in the Anglican Church at any rate, people assume you mean clergy or monks or nuns or 'missionaries' (or possibly doctors, nurses and one or two other of the professions). We really have no notion at all of vocation for the ordinary Christian.

I used to do a bit of teaching in an Anglican theological college. In a course on vocation I asked a group of students to reflect silently for a few minutes on the question: 'What have you done in your life up to now; what have you seen as your Christian ministry?' They came up with: running a youth group, leading a prayer and Bible study group, preaching, teaching in Sunday school, visiting hospital patients, befriending newcomers to the church, presenting Jesus to individuals, healing, leading worship, and being available to people who want to sound off. These are all worthwhile activities, but they did sound to me very like a list of the vicar's duties. If this is what we mean by Christian ministry it amounts to little more than sharing out the ordained minister's job.

When we began to dig a little deeper in that student group we found that some of them did feel that the jobs they had done before coming to theological college had offered opportunities for Christian ministry, though they had not thought of it in that way. One had worked as a research chemist. He became concerned about the frustration felt in his department because they knew little of how their work fitted into the long-term objectives of the company. He made representations to the management about this. He said he would not have done this had he not been a Christian. Another had worked in an income tax office. He said that he remembered dealing with a man with a complicated tax problem more sympathetically than he would have done if he had not been a Christian. Those sounded a bit vague and unfocused as we talked. They need not have done. What they were talking about was the humanising of institutions. If there was vagueness in my discussion with the students it was because of the weakness of our conception of what Christian ministry might be.

Sometimes lip service is paid from pulpits and other such places to a wider vision of what Christian ministry might be. But before the resounding phrases have ceased to echo around, another message can be heard whispering up and down the aisles: that the people in the pews are *lay* people, which writes their status off at a stroke as the non-professionals, the non-experts, and by implication the people without a specific vocation beyond the general one 'to be a Christian'. The words lay person and laity should be expunged from the Christian vocabulary! They may have a hallowed origin, but I am afraid our notion of what the laos (the people of God) is to be has become emasculated beyond the point of no return.

This clerical hijacking of the notion of vocation is thus enshrined in our language, which makes it particularly difficult to see it any other way. Small wonder that the full-time sacred ministry is seen as the only outlet for the average Christian with a desire for service and self-giving.

Let me try to clarify the notion of vocation a little. I think it is helpful to notice three different senses of the word. First there is your personal or unique vocation, the approach to which I have been trying to outline in this book.

Secondly there is the general calling or invitation to be a Christian, to be a follower of Christ. Sometimes the word vocation or calling is used in this very wide sense. For example St Paul always uses it to mean this. This is the general invitation to be a Christian and does not imply any particular task or job.

The third sense in which it is used denotes the call of God to a role or 'other-defined' task, where the calling of God is mediated through the Church and not as it were on a personal hot line from heaven. The most obvious example of institutional vocation is the call to be ordained. I say 'most obvious' but I am bound to add that that is more an expression of hope than a fact! In reality the Church (and here I only presume to speak of the Anglican Church) is extremely muddled about this. Most Anglicans would not think of the call to be ordained as a call to a role or an other-defined task. They think of it in terms of personal calling, in other words in terms of the first sense of the word. They think that the call of God to be ordained comes from within a person, and that all the Church has to do is to endorse it. And a great many people who think their inner sense of calling should lead to ordination are devastated when they are not recommended for training for ordination by ABM, the department of the Church of England which has responsibility for selection.

This muddle, and the hurt it causes many people, is in my opinion unnecessary. But it does have a longish history and there are many factors that have contributed to it. It will be a huge task for the Church to unscramble it. It is not my intention to go into how we have arrived in the muddle and what keeps us here (I say more about this in my book *Called or Collared?*), except to say that the first question that is put to candidates for ordination in the Anglican ordination service does not help. 'Do you believe', asks the bishop, 'so far as you know your own heart, that God has called you to the office and work of a priest in his Church?' We have no business to ask that question, and before the sixteenth century it was not asked. The first step towards unscrambling the muddle would be to remove it.

Let me explain what I mean by saying that the call to be ordained is a call to a role. Being a vicar is basically an other-defined job, in the sense I described in Chapter 2. The Church needs certain tasks doing for it in order to keep Church communities and congregations true to their nature, true to what the Church is for; in other words to prevent them turning into something else. That is a job, a chore even, that any community or institution needs doing for it if it is to have any continuity of purpose. If not, it will lose its sense of purpose or become something different. In the case of the Church the tasks required are things like teaching, leading worship, and 'modelling' the Christian life. Those are the basic duties for which it requires candidates. A person chosen for this does not need an inward sense of vocation to those particular tasks. What he or she does need are the right qualities for those tasks. That is why the choice needs to be made by others, by the duly appointed representatives of the institution. The Church in effect says to a person 'you are called by God to be ordained'. Thus the calling of God comes, not on a personal hot line, but via the Church. Initially it might come through the suggestion of your vicar or other people in your congregation. But eventually the Church's choice will be formally expressed at the ordination service.

When it comes to actually doing the job you may or may not feel an inner sense of calling to it, or to some parts of the job and not others. But there is a sense in which whether you feel that or not is irrelevant. There is no reason why you should not, but it is not *required*. That is to say, it is not required that you feel an inner sense of calling *to the particular tasks to be done by a clergyperson*.

But if you are ordained you do need an inner sense of vocation in *some* aspect of your activities. I believe it is essential that candidates for ordination should be people who are consciously responding to God's personal call to them in some area of their life. It might be in some task outside anything remotely resembling ministerial or priestly activity: or it might be in some part of the vicar's job. What is essential for such candidates is that they have begun to discover their personal calling in the first sense described above. I believe that to be a basic requirement for any Christian. Therefore the vicar needs to be living her response to God's personal calling of her *because she is a Christian*, and not just because she is ordained. Her living of it as an ordained person is part of her modelling of a Christian life that is for everyone. So, for example, if the vicar's personal vocation is in starting a counselling service for people with AIDS and their families, he will do that as a private individual, not because he is vicar of a parish. In fact some of his parishioners may not be too keen on him doing it, and in his position as vicar he will have to explain what he does and why he does it. In doing so, if he is a truly called person, there will shine out from him love and enthusiasm and giftedness for this work. He will be modelling a style of life and activity that should be part of every Christian's existence.

Conversely, if the vicar is not living her personal calling in some part of her life, she will tend to block the members of her congregation discovering theirs. Unless a vicar (or anyone else for that matter) is finding fulfilment exercising his gift, his personal call, he will tend to prevent others doing so. There does seem to be a dog-in-the-manger dynamic that tends to operate when a person is not, at least in some aspect of their life, doing what they are for. There is always envy skulking around in such a person that may cause them, whether they are unaware of it or not, to resent or even to hinder other people finding and responding to their personal vocation.

If all this is right you may be wondering why so many people feel an inward sense of calling to be ordained. I believe it is because that feeling is for some people the beginning, the first sign, of a personal calling. A personal calling tends to appear first in a fairly vague and undifferentiated form, like 'I want to be more whole-hearted in what I do' or 'I want to live a more committed Christian life' or 'I want to be a person of God' or 'I want to work with people'. There is a great deal of work to be done between that and moving out on a focused call, as I have tried to explain. But meanwhile the vicar or priest or minister is around as a ready-made model of whole-hearted discipleship, of committed Christian living, a person of God working with people. And it must be said that in so far as there are other models of whole-hearted Christian life, they tend to be either born-again fundamentalists or are pretty hidden and are often not given much encouragement by the Church. We badly need other models of committed Christian life that are not clerical or ecclesiastical or fundamentalist but are nevertheless thoroughly full-blooded about Christian living.

I hope I have managed to explain this clearly. It is sometimes quite difficult to get hold of, because what we live as a Church (as least in the Anglican Church) is so opposite to this. I have to admit that it has taken me all of thirty years to begin to see it, and even now I am only beginning to get it clear. Perhaps that is because I was for a long time vicar of a parish myself. There were many things I disliked about that job and I just assumed it was because I was a miserable sinner and that I ought to like them. I think I see now that it does not matter whether you like them or not. Someone has to do them, for the sake of the health of the Church. But there does need to be an important part of your daily activity that you do like, that it is a joy to do. If there is not some reasonable balance between chore activities and joy activities, your soul begins to wither. And that is not only disastrous for the vicar. It is also a disaster for the whole congregation.

I have said all this to provide a background for suggesting six ways in which I believe the Church could help people discover their personal vocation and get into action.

1. *By being aware that activities beyond the bounds of Sunday and the church building are a vital part of Christian ministry.* I have come across many people, deeply committed in their daily work, who feel that the Church does not see what they do in any sense as Christian activity. I think for example of a senior trade union official who had been moved to a new area. On the Sunday following his move he went to the local church. After the service he introduced himself to the vicar and offered the use of his experience and expertise. The vicar asked him if he would be a magazine distributor! Many people feel that the Church not only has no interest in what they do, but also precious little awareness of the needs of people who 'battle with the structures' in their daily life.

2. *By reducing the number of local church clubs and societies which prevent engagement with the two journeys.* I mean the sort which meet monthly to hear speakers on dog training or 'My holiday in Transylvania'. There is a polite clapping at the end, and after tea, biscuits and gossip we all go home. This kind of thing might seem harmless enough. But in my view it actively prevents people getting to grips with the two journeys, and organisations like this do tend to suck other people into them, as though they were the be-all and end-all of the Church's weekday life. One aspect of the inward journey for a congregation is the building up of genuine community and sharing. Meetings run in this kind of way

actually *prevent* that. At best they keep the human contacts to the formal and the uninvolved; at worst, they offer opportunities for gossip and character assassination. Neither do such societies encourage action in any significant way. It is almost as though they keep people in suspended animation, in a sort of no man's land that seems designed to prevent both genuine community and lively action. You might ask why people go? It reminds me of Schopenhauer's porcupines. They huddle together in the winter to try and keep out the cold, but not too close lest they hurt one another with their spines.

3. *By clergy living their personal call as well as their institutional one.* I hope I have already said enough for it to be clear why I think this is important. The clergy are pivotal people in a congregation. Just as people grow to be like their dogs, so do congregations mirror the strengths and weaknesses of their minister or vicar. One of the creeping horrors of being vicar of the same parish for a lot of years is that as you stand out there on a Sunday morning you gradually begin to see the reflection of your own face! It is crucial that the clergy provide adequate models of the Christian life, and that they exercise their gifts in freedom so that others can be free to exercise theirs.

4. *By the selection procedures for ordination requiring that candidates be people who are already living their personal call to some degree.* In other words, before they are even considered for ordination, candidates should have done some mature work on their inner sense of call which has issued in conscious action. I believe that living your call in some area of your activity should be regarded as a part of the ordinary Christian's life. What I am suggesting is that ordination candidates should be fully Christian in this way. I realise this is crying for the moon. But I do not see much change taking place in our congregations until it happens much more commonly. Because even if the people in the pews want to do something that will lead in this sort of direction, it is

very easily squashed by the vicar. People then either give up in a docile way, or leave the Church and try to do something on their own.

5. *By providing a structure for encouraging and checking people's inner sense of call.* I have in mind the kind of thing I suggested at the end of Chapter 1, a small group of people in a congregation who are willing to work at the two journeys in their own life and encourage each other. I enlarged on this in Chapter 13 in the quotation from the Quakers' *Church Government*. Let me quote again from that:

> The importance of the local worshipping group in fostering concerned service cannot be over-estimated. Where members know one another well and watch over one another for good, each is encouraged to use his gifts in obedience to the inward Guide. This obedience, habitually practised, is the source from which Concerns spring. It also gives to the sensitive the power to recognise a nascent Concern and to distinguish between the true Concern and a momentary enthusiasm or a good idea. A timely word from an experienced Friend may bring another Friend to awareness of a divine leading or help him to accept that a particular desire to serve may be a true call even though the service envisaged is also attractive. Mutual confidence and understanding lead naturally to readiness to share potential Concerns with the group, and enable a Friend to accept restraint as well as to rejoice in the group's sanction and support. (para. 867)

The Quakers go beyond this and provide machinery for checking out a person's sense of call at a wider level than a local congregation, including the provision of a 'minute of authorisation' should it be approved. In Anglican terms that might be trying to run before we can walk. I have visions of heavy-handed church committees squashing all sorts of creative initiatives, until

such time as their members have been sufficiently per-
meated with this expectant attitude of mind and this
level of openness to God. But even little groups in congregations would be a start.

6. *By having local commissioning services for called people.*
There is public recognition for the ordained ministry
which finds expression in public worship. Why not for
other kinds of ministry? It would need to be tailormade
for each occasion, rather than some standard, ritualised
form. But it could be a very short affair, taking its place
as part of the Sunday worship. This would help both
the called person and the congregation to a much wider
and much more explicit notion of what Christian ministry might be. As it became commoner you would begin
to have a much better appreciation of what other people
in your congregation see as their ministry. You would
begin to see the tremendous richness of the corporate
ministry of the Church in society through its members,
which is often so hidden. If commissioning at a service
seems inappropriate, think of some other way of making
known what 'called' people do, and giving support to
them.

Two exercises follow, to help you forward in relation to
items 5 and 6.

TWO EXERCISES

1. Start a sharing group in your church or district. If you use
the exercises from this book as a resource from time to time,
consult the Appendix to begin with. The aim of the group
will be to help you and the other members to make progress
on the inward and outward journeys. As the group life
develops you might like to introduce the notion of accountability. For example, if a group member becomes aware that
an important issue for her is building some times of silence
into her daily routine, she might ask the group to hold her
accountable for doing something about it. The others would
then encourage her to set herself a practical and achievable

objective in this matter for the next few weeks. She could then report back each week how she got on, not so that the others can pass judgment, but as a way of helping herself to incorporate into her life the values that she wants to embody. It can be a great aid to a wobbly will to lay it on the line in this way. The group's main job is to listen and encourage.

Different members may want to be accountable for very different kinds of things. Usually a person will want to be held accountable for something they want to build into their life, but know they have difficulty with it. Items might be as widely different as prayer, or relationships, or a person's attitude to herself, or some piece of action. One of the things I have at times asked to be held accountable for is fun! I can easily become over-serious and over-involved with work. In the early stages it will be important for members to choose their own things to be accountable for. They will discover in practice as the months go by whether they have chosen accurately or practicably. But as you get to know and accept each other and become aware of each one's developing journey, you may be able to help each other to a greater clarity about what the issues are in your life at present that need grappling with in this way. In time, over months or years, your group will be able to do what I described in my fifth suggestion in this chapter – be a seed-bed and a check point for personal vocation.

2. Ask your local church to commission you for the piece of work that you see as your God-given task at present. You would need to get together with one or two others to devise some simple form for doing this. You could incorporate it into the Sunday worship in a suitable way. Alternatively you could suggest that another member of your congregation might be commissioned for their God-given task.

Even if you think your requests will not be agreed to, it will help to get discussion of what Christian ministry might be on to the agenda of your church.

A PARABLE

I remembered one morning when I discovered a cocoon in the bark of a tree, just as the butterfly was making a hole in its case and preparing to come out. I waited a while, but it was too long appearing and I was impatient. I bent over it and breathed on it to warm it. I warmed it as quickly as I could and the miracle began to happen before my eyes, faster than life. The case opened, the butterfly started slowly crawling out and I shall never forget my horror when I saw how its wings were folded back and crumpled. The wretched butterfly tried with its whole trembling body to unfold them. Bending over it, I tried to help it with my breath. In vain. It needed to be hatched out patiently and the unfolding of the wings should be a gradual process in the sun. Now it was too late. My breath had forced the butterfly to appear, all crumpled before its time. It struggled desperately, and a few seconds later, died in the palm of my hand.

That little body is, I do believe, the greatest weight I have on my conscience. For I realize today that it is a mortal sin to violate the great laws of nature. We should not hurry, we should not be impatient, but we should confidently obey the eternal rhythm.

I sat on a rock to absorb this New Year's thought. Ah, if only that little butterfly could always flutter before me to show me the way. (Nikos Kazantsakis, *Zorba the Greek*, Bruno Cassirer, 1959, pp. 129–30)

17

Counting the Cost

In the mid-1960s I read *The True Wilderness* by Harry
Williams. It was for me a breath of life. Jesus was presented as a human being, not some superhuman figure
playing at being human. According to Williams it was
permissible for a Christian to be human, too. What a relief!
We weren't required to crush our humanity, but to enter
into it more deeply and generously.

As I write this it is Lent. Harry Williams was particularly
scornful about the widespread misuse of this season. 'It is
a pity that we think of Lent as a time when we try to make
ourselves uncomfortable in some fiddling but irritating
way. And it's more than a pity, it's a tragic disaster, that
we also think of it as a time to indulge in... a good
orthodox grovel to a pseudo-Lord, the pharisee in each of
us we call God and who despises the rest of what we are.'
The way people observe Lent he called 'disguised self-
idolatry'. At that time, this was quite a revolutionary
message for many Christians. To me it was releasing and
life-giving!

But if we are to enter into our humanity more deeply
and generously, there is a price to be paid, a real one, not
just some minor self-chosen discomfort. I have referred to
this here and there in previous chapters, but I think the
question of the cost needs a chapter of its own to give it
the prominence it should have in relation to the other

aspects of the discernment of personal calling. Besides, it's an excuse for me to include one of my favourite stories, the Iranian fairy tale which concludes this section, a very powerful parable of the journey of responding to God's personal calling to you. It is full of symbolism: of the need for self-awareness (the mirror); of wholeness (e.g. the roundness of the bath) and the risks associated with seeking it; of the necessity of finding your own way where there is no ready-made path; of the need to kill off the spirit of imitation (i.e. your way will have something unique about it – the parrot here stands specifically for the spirit of imitation); and though you yourself will need to exert every ounce of effort and of wisdom to travel this road, it is actually God who will, through you, bring out of it new life for others.

There has been much misinterpretation of the meaning of Lent and of self-denial. In the gospel of Matthew, Chapter 16, Jesus says: 'If any want to become my followers, let them deny themselves and take up their cross and follow me.' In this sentence Jesus gives us three injunctions, each of which has been seriously misunderstood.

I said a little about the first one, self-denial, in Chapter 6. The misunderstanding centres on what 'self' is to be renounced and denied. I have been at some pains in this book to explain that God calls you to discover the self you truly are, that greater and fuller self you could become, and to let it flower generously in some particular activity at God's invitation. Self-denial most definitely does not mean nipping that process in the bud. Interpreting it that way is a cop-out, an act of cowardice, a frightened refusal to live. Heaven knows, many of us are tempted to that at times – 'anything for a quiet life!' But in our heart of hearts we know it is an excuse and an evasion. We long for life, but are deeply afraid of it as well.

But there is a genuine kind of self-denial which is very necessary if you are to be responsive to God. Living more deeply and generously and allowing the flowering of what you could become and could do does carry a price. It may mean losing friends, or your good name, or status, or power, or security; all the things TV advertisers try to persuade us we cannot live without. It *will* mean denying the self that runs after or clings to these things. That part of our makeup that we call our ego will need to be demoted, diminished, and in the end done away with. That can be very painful indeed: but it is not destructive. On the contrary, it is part of the flowering, the letting go that is essential if we are to be genuinely open to God's prompting.

Jesus' second injunction is 'Take up your cross'. This could be taken to mean something like 'select your cross'. But the cross is not something you choose. The cross is what is liable to happen to you if you set out to respond to God's calling and get into action. Jesus' untrammelled creative response to God in his teaching and dealings with people was a threat to those who thought power, and influence, and status, and money, and toeing the line, were the most important things in life. We too can expect to be a threat to others, as we begin to live what we are born for with growing freedom. I think of a friend who is very able in her job, with quite a flair for dealing with the 'people issues' which are a central part of it. But because she exercises her giftedness in this way she is a threat to her manager, who deals with it by undermining and blocking her. You may remember that in Chapter 27 of his gospel St Matthew comments: 'Pilate knew that it was out of envy that they handed Jesus over.' When a person is not doing what they are for, envy will be stirred up in them when they encounter someone who is. It may not be conscious, but it is always there. Somewhere in our inner depths we know that there is more to life than kudos, and power, and money, and all the rest of it, but we resist that knowledge for fear of the demands it might make. Envy *can* be used constructively, as I suggested in Chapter 10. But unheeded and untended it can work all sorts of hidden devilry.

We have already thought about Jesus' third injunction 'follow me' at some length in Chapter 6. Properly understood, it is an invitation to life, to a fuller life, you might say, than any of us have a right to expect. We do not have a right to it, of course. It is a gift, a rich and lavish present offered for the taking. And in taking it we ourselves become a gift to others.

Jesus tells a cautionary tale in Chapter 14 of Luke's gospel: 'Which of you here, intending to build a tower, would not first sit down and work out the cost to see if he had enough to complete it? Otherwise, if he laid the foundation and found himself unable to finish the work, the onlookers would all start making fun of him and saying, "here is a man who started to build and was unable to finish".' It is a rather practical and down to earth warning about the cost of truly living.

AN EXERCISE

Your journey to fulfilment and fruitfulness may require of you some letting go, some sacrifice, possibly even some hardship.

What might prevent you from travelling this road?

What do you need to let go of?

A PARABLE

A great and noble prince receives orders from his king to investigate the mysterious Bath of Badgerd. When he approaches it, having gone through many dangerous adventures, he hears that nobody ever returned from it: but he insists on going on. He is received at a round building by a barber with a mirror who leads him into the bath; but as soon as the prince enters the water, a thunderous noise breaks out, it gets completely dark, the barber disappears, and slowly the water begins to rise.

The prince swims desperately round until the water finally reaches the top of the round cupola which forms the roof of the bath. Now he fears he is lost; but he says a prayer and grasps the centre-stone of the cupola. Again a thunderous noise, everything changes, and he stands alone in a desert.

After long and painful wandering, he comes upon a beautiful garden in the middle of which is a circle of stone statues. In the centre of the statues he sees a parrot in its cage, and a voice from above says to him: 'O hero, you will probably not escape alive from this bath. Once, Gay-omart, the First Man, found an enormous diamond that shone more brightly than the sun or moon. He decided to hide it where no one could find it; and therefore he built this magical bath in order to protect it. The parrot you see here forms part of the magic. At its feet lie a golden bow and arrows on a golden chain. With them you may try three times to shoot the parrot. If you hit him the curse will be lifted; if not, you will be petrified, as were all these other people.'

The prince tries once; and fails. His legs turn to stone. He takes the most careful aim and shoots a second time; and misses. He is petrified up to his chest. The third time he just shuts his eyes exclaiming 'God is great!', shoots blindly, and this time hits the parrot. An outbreak of thunder and clouds of dust! When this has subsided, in place of the parrot is an enormous, beautiful diamond, and all the statues have come to life again.

Iranian fairy tale

Postscript

I said in Chapter 1 that the process I have outlined is not
linear, to be gone through once so that you emerge at
the end with complete clarity about your sense of direction.
The present-day cult of instant and effortless answers is
very unhelpful in this. Nor is this process a painless sol-
ution to the world's ills – 'take two milligrams a day and
in your battle against the dead hand of tradition you will
be protected against the slings and arrows of the frightened
or the vicious'. Individuals and institutions resist change
actively, not just through inertia. We human beings wage
war against life. We are as deeply afraid of living as of
dying. So the journey that is offered is neither speedy nor
pain-free. But it does lead to life – for you, and sometimes,
through you, for others.

Appendix

THINGS TO NOTE IF YOU ARE THINKING OF USING
THIS BOOK IN A GROUP

Some advantages

1. It will give you an opportunity to share your experience of
   each exercise with others. It is valuable to hear yourself say
   aloud what you experienced in the exercise, to read aloud
   what you wrote in your journal (or as much as you feel
   comfortable with). Laying it on the line like that helps to
   encourage you to own and to value your experience and your
   feelings about things, even though it will require of you a
   little courage now and then. Being listened to attentively and
   receptively by others also aids that process.
2. Meeting with others on a regular agreed basis can firm up
   your resolve to do the exercises and to stick with the process.
3. You will hear how other people experienced each exercise,
   which will almost certainly be different.
4. As the weeks pass you will get to know one another at quite
   a deep level. It will become possible for you to encourage and
   support and, where appropriate, challenge one another much
   more appropriately and in ways much more suited to each
   individual.

Some suggestions

In whatever way you advertise or convene the group, make sure
the dates, times, and place of meeting are clear and that everyone
who wants to join can manage them. Meeting in someone's home
is best, if that is possible. Emphasise that the course depends on
the commitment of each person to come to every session, to
arrive in time to start at the agreed time, and to do the individual
work (to see the crucial importance of this, look again at the

second paragraph of p. 156). If because of some unforeseen eventuality someone misses a session, they need to take responsibility for being up to date with the individual work. Each participant also needs to be aware that this process they are joining in involves learning by doing, and does not rely on the expertise of a leader. Each person needs to take responsibility for their own learning. This also requires that every participant keeps a journal of some kind and does each exercise with pen and paper. This is really the only way to allow what you learn for yourself to take root in your life. Neglecting the use of pen and paper is a way of avoiding learning anything.

It is probably best to read the chapter and do its exercise each time *before* coming to the group meeting. The task of the meeting will then primarily be for each person to share what happened as they did the exercise and what they found. (Before coming to the very first meeting everyone should also have read the appendix. At your very first meeting you might want to start off with the exercise on p. 198.)

You could start each session with a simple meal, with each member, or pair of members, taking turns to provide it. I suggest the meal be simple, so that it doesn't become competitive!

When the meal is over and cleared away, it might be a good idea to have some time of silence, some way of letting go of the activities and concerns of the day, and becoming centred and 'present'.

Then have the sharing time. A good number for a sharing group is four. If there are more people on the course you will need to divide up. I suggest each group should not be less than three or more than five. It helps to build up trust and openness if the membership of the groups is the same each time you meet. The more the groups change, the more superficial will be the sharing.

Depending on the amount of time you have for the sharing group(s) at your meeting, you could also each have a turn to share what struck you in the reading matter in the chapter, or in the 'story'.

At some point in the evening one of you could read a suitable quotation from my book *Invitations: God's calling for everyone*, which was originally designed as an anthology of quotes and stories to accompany the *Live for a Change* process (the sections are not all in the same order, but it could be quite useful to use as something to mine things from) – or use a suitable quote of your own.

You might end with brief prayers. You could use a Taizé chant, or a record of some suitable music.

It needs someone to take responsibility for some of the afore-mentioned items. I think it is best to take turns in this. You could each take a turn to be responsible for one task each evening, so that, as far as possible, everyone is able to contribute something to the evening.

This new edition of *Live for a Change* has 17 chapters and 17 exercises. You may feel you do not wish to go through the whole book in one go. There might be something to be said for doing Chapters 1–10 in one series; and then, after a gap of weeks or months, meeting for another series to do 11–17. I do think it is important to do the complete process, because the whole point of it is to help you to *link* the inward and the outward. But many of us, in beginning to work at the inward, realise that there is more to do and to follow up than we thought. It *can* be premature to rush on too quickly to the outward direction: though I should add that I have taken careful account of this point in the way I have done the second half of the book. There should be no problem in going straight on without a break, if you wish to. Participants will be able to find their own level.

Some guidelines

If you want to give the group a chance it is very important that:

a. *every* member of the group does each exercise and is willing to share their experience of doing so. Having passengers, or 'non-playing members', or people who think they have 'done it all before', will kill the group stone dead. For the members to be able to foster one another's growth it is essential that they are all there on the same terms, with a willingness to listen, and a willingness to share when your turn comes.

b. the place where you meet is conducive to the process, comfort-able and welcoming, and *guaranteed* to be free of extraneous interruptions. If freedom from interruptions and distractions is not guaranteed, the attention of everyone on the task is unlikely. It is a recipe for increasing frustration, superficiality and avoidance of the task.

c. the chairs are arranged so that each of you can easily see the others in your group (sofas can be unhelpful, where people are sitting side by side rather than face to face). For example, if there are four in a group – which is a good number for sharing – it is best to set the chairs out in the shape of a maltese cross.

d. members are aware of the difference between 'sharing' (i.e. having an uninterrupted opportunity to tell of their experience in doing an exercise), and discussion (where opinions are passed, where there is general free-for-all talk about the rightness or wrongness of what happens, expression of views about what ought to happen or what people ought to think, theorising about what might have happened, etc.). Be clear that the group is meeting for the purpose of 'sharing'.

e. at each meeting, before you start, you agree on how much time is available for 'sharing'. Divide that time by the number of members in the group (or in each group if there is more than one). E.g., if one hour is available and there are four in the group, 15 minutes is the maximum time allowable for each individual. While a person is sharing, the person on their right keeps an eye on the time and makes sure s/he does not go beyond their allotted time. This helps to curb the ones who might hog the time and to encourage the quieter ones. It also gives everyone a stake in the discipline of your time together. A person is not of course compelled to take all the time allotted to them. But if a member seems to dry up before their time is up, take a little time to be silent and expectant in case anything else occurs to them.

f. when it is your turn to share, do not feel you *have* to 'tell all': say as much as you feel comfortable with. As the weeks go by and trust grows, find the courage to say more: that will give encouragement to others.

g. avoid the preacher's pronoun ('we', as in 'we think . . .', 'we do . . .', 'we feel . . .', etc.) like the plague! See below, p. 198

h. when another person is having their turn to share, the rest need to *listen*, giving their whole attention to them; where it seems appropriate encourage the person to put into words their experience of the exercise and what it has brought to the surface, the feelings, hopes, longings, fears, etc. (There is more about the process of listening later on in this appendix, *which needs to be read carefully before your course starts.*)

i. regard what is said in your group as confidential, not to be spoken of to anyone outside the group.

j. when there is noticeable or persistent disregard of the foregoing guidelines, someone must find a suitable way of reminding – if necessary confronting – the offender. Letting it continue will hinder the development of the group. The bit of pain or risk involved is well worthwhile for the health and growth of the group and its members.

One other point needs making. When the group is initially proposed or convened, it does need to be made clear that it is not a therapy group. The people who come need to be capable of taking responsibility for themselves, people who are reasonably well-functioning in their daily life and work. If someone is being treated for depression, or some other psychiatric or emotional problem, it is too much to expect them to be able to cope with what a process like this may stir up. It is no kindness to them or the other group members to encourage them to join.

The importance of listening
This will be such an important make-or-break factor in your group life that I want to say quite a lot more about it, and to suggest a couple of exercises that focus on learning to listen which you might care to build into your group life at suitable points.

When I was in parish work I used to spend time calling on people in their homes. One day someone was telling me about her life. It was late afternoon and my thoughts must have begun to stray to my next port of call, teatime at home. 'Am I boring you, Vicar?' she asked suddenly.

I remember another occasion at the vicarage. I had received some bad news and was feeling a bit stunned. Someone however was booked to come and see me that morning. I had a desperate struggle to put the worry aside and give my attention to that person as they talked about their situation.

Sometimes it is extraneous factors like that, nothing to do with the person you are listening to, which tug at your attention. At other times it is things the person says that send you off on a train of thought of your own, or which trigger feelings in you which then colour what you hear and what you say. For example, a person may start telling me about a situation in their parish, and may have some critical things to say about their vicar. I begin to feel that I could easily have done what he did and the wish to defend him (me!) rises within me. If I am going to listen openly to what this person in front of me is feeling, I will need to be aware of my own stirrings in a background way and consciously set them aside.

Genuine listening means giving the other person time and 'space' to express what they want. In practice that means two things. First, it means setting aside your own feelings and thoughts so that the other has the freedom to give expression to how s/he feels. This may mean taking time on some other occasion to deal with your own feelings with someone who can listen to you. There are times when we all need a listening ear. Secondly it means giving some signals that you are receiving, that is, accepting into yourself, what s/he is saying. That of course can be done by your facial expression and general demeanour. But it helps if every so often at suitable points you summarise what they have said, not just the factual content, but especially the feelings that they have expressed. When that is done accurately it gives the speaker a marvellous sense that they are being listened to, and they will have the feeling that they have a bit of space to explore their feelings. True listening of this sort is a kind of hospitality.

Let me give you an example. Someone might say: 'I like doing things for my husband and children and I really enjoy the time we spend together. In some ways I don't regret giving up going to work, but I do sometimes find housework rather boring. I had always thought that I would find motherhood totally satisfying and fulfilling. But sometimes I wonder if there is something more for me than that. I really don't know.'

Here are some responses a listener might make:

1. 'You sound to me like a typical bored housewife.'
2. 'My wife stayed at home when the children were young.'
3. 'You sound really happy to me. I think you should be really thankful for what you've got.'
4. 'It sounds as though you feel really fulfilled at home; but having to do the chores makes you wonder if there is more to you than being a wife and mother.'

The first response is made by a middle-aged divorcée; the second by an older man; the third by a widow; the fourth person managed to set aside her own feelings and attitudes and conveyed that she heard and received what the speaker actually said. You can see how each of the first three responses is coloured by the experience of the person who said it; they did not really hear what the speaker said.

So when you meet to share how you found these exercises, struggle with this discipline of listening to one another. For example, when someone is talking about something they have drawn give the person space to explore their feelings about it, which they may not have put into words before. 'I don't know what I think until I hear what I say' goes the proverb. Give the speaker 'permission' to look for words to put to their experience in the way I have suggested. The whole point of these exercises is to help you to become more aware of things which may at first be shadowy or vague or unclear. It is therefore vital that the other people in your group do not get in the way of this delicate process.

So may I offer some do's and don't's for when you are speaking and when you are listening?

When you are listening:
Do look at the person you are listening to.
Do be aware of how they feel in what they are saying.
Do accept the factuality of their experience, even if it makes you feel uncomfortable or you wish it were otherwise. They know better than you do what they feel.
Do keep your own feelings and opinions to yourself.
Do ask 'what' or 'how' questions if you think this will help the speaker further to articulate what they feel.
Do try now and then to articulate that you have heard what the person is saying.
Don't interrupt.
Don't ask 'why' questions.
Don't pass judgment, if possible not even in your own heart!
Don't give advice.
Don't make theories about why the other person feels as they do, even if *they themselves* want to!
Don't convey to the speaker that their experience ought to have been different.
Don't look for 'problems' to sort out.

When it is your turn to share your experience of the exercise:

Do say what happened as you did it, how you found it, what feelings it prompted.
Do be honest in what you choose to say.
Do find the courage to say what *you* feel; try and keep to your personal experience.
Do try and find words for what may not yet be clear and distinct.
You don't have to tell all, just what you feel comfortable with.

Don't take refuge in theorising or talking about ideas.

Don't be afraid to speak when you are not clear about how you feel, or when you feel it might be inconsistent.

Don't worry if sometimes you feel you have said too much. That is sometimes a sign that you have given generously of yourself. It will usually have been a help to the others, as you may discover later.

Both when you are speaker *and* when you are listener: Avoid 'we' statements like the plague *unless you make it quite clear who 'we' refers to.* 'We' often really means 'I' or 'you', but shirks the responsibility of saying so plainly. At best it is making an unwarranted assumption about what 'everyone' feels. At worst it can sound like smugness or preaching.

You will sometimes notice that it is not only you that does not always keep to these do's and don't's. Look for some appropriate way of drawing attention to persistent unhelpful contravention of them. If necessary, say it plainly. It may cause a bit of pain; but then growth seldom happens without pain. If you consistently avoid the pain, you will avoid the growth.

You may feel that all this is beyond you, that you cannot be bothered to go into it with this amount of care. But reflect for a moment. Listening to another person requires the same set of qualities and disciplines as openness to God. Both require receptiveness and a willingness to let go of the steering wheel. So the one is good practice for the other. And the advantage of learning to listen to other people is that it is easier to check out how we are doing. It is much easier to kid ourselves that we are growing in openness to God; and much less easy to check out. So if you are meeting in a group the need to listen is not just a tiresome extra, it is an opportunity to work at a vital aspect of what this book is about.

TWO EXERCISES

When you first meet as a group

Let it be somewhere comfortable and informal. If you have all read this appendix before you come, you may be feeling a bit daunted. So take some time first to feel at ease with one another. Sit so that each person can comfortably see the others. Introduce yourselves to one another. Give everyone an opportunity to say a bit about themselves. Then give everyone a chance to say a little about why they are interested in using this book and in meeting together, what their hopes are, and whether they have any apprehensions.

When you feel reasonably at home with one another (which might be at your second meeting if you are taking your time), you might take turns to share your experience of the 'hats' exercise in Chapter 1. *Make sure each person has a proper turn.* Don't do it as a free-for-all. While a person has her turn, the others listen and give the person unhurried space to share what they wish.

At some later stage in your series of meetings, you may feel the need of a more focused listening exercise. What follows is one way to do it.

At a subsequent meeting
This exercise is really best done in groups of four, so that everyone has a clear task at each stage. You could do it with three, and have just one observer. If you were to try it with six it would make rather a marathon of it, but would not be imposs- ible with four people acting as observers each time. However I will describe it on the assumption that four people are involved.

First have five minutes or so of silence while each of you makes a brief list of things – interests, activities, beliefs, and so on – that are waning in your life; and a list of things that are growing in importance, emerging, coming to be. Choose at least one item from each list that you would be happy to share your feelings about.

When everyone has chosen something suitable in this way, sit yourselves in fours, so that you are facing one another like the four points of the compass. Each member will then have a turn to be speaker, listener and observer. When it is your turn to speak, sit facing the person whose turn it is to listen. The listener's task is to listen and to help the speaker to articulate her or his feelings about their situation. The best way to do this is not to ask questions or make comments. At suitable points simply convey in words that you have heard not just the factual content of what the speaker is saying, but also the feelings about it that the speaker has put into words. At its most basic, this is simply choosing appropriate moments to say back in a very abridged and summary form what you have heard, paying particular attention to the feelings that have been expressed, but not to the ones that have not! There are no prizes for delving: and there need to be penalties for any attempt to interpret, or to discover *why* the person feels as they do! That is making theories; you may find that satisfying for yourself, but it is not listening.

Do not worry if this approach feels a bit stilted at first. It probably will. But with practice and sensitivity it can be a very unobtrusive and effective way of giving a person space to express themselves, to be themselves. True listening is a kind of hospitality, a place of genuine welcome and concern for an individual's needs and feelings. Listening requires warmth and interest, but not intrusiveness or inquisitiveness. It requires receptivity, but not unresponsive passivity, and to quite a large extent it is a discipline that can be learnt.

The other two members are not to speak but to observe the conversation. One is to focus their attention particularly on the speaker. Does s/he seem to have the freedom to say what s/he wishes, or does s/he seem constrained and limited or even stopped mid-sentence by the listener's interjections? Notice the points in the conversation when their responses seem to enable them to say more, and when they seem to have the opposite effect. The other observer is to focus on the listener. Does s/he listen? Does s/he check back accurately what s/he hears, or does what s/he says mirror her own concerns rather than the speaker's? Does s/he register accurately the level and nature of the feelings expressed by the speaker at different points; does s/he for example reflect mild irritation as anger, or embarrassment as fright or deep sadness as a temporary disappointment? Does s/he register how the speaker is feeling now in this conversation with these people observing? If it is relevant, does s/he reflect it back appropriately to enable the person to feel free to speak?

You probably need to allow the conversation to run for some seven to ten minutes to give it a chance to get under way. One of the observers could act as timekeeper. At the end of that time, the listener and the speaker may be 'debriefed' by their observers in a discussion among the four of you. The observers first give a chance to the listener and the speaker to share any reactions they have. Did the speaker subjectively *feel* listened to? That is an important touchstone. How did the listener feel as s/he struggled with the discipline of listening? In this discussion, the observers can share their own observations at appropriate points. After five minutes or so of this, or longer if you need it, swap roles, and do the whole process again. The aim of the exercise is to give each person a turn at being listener, so the whole process needs to be gone through four times. But it has the twin aim of offering each person as the speaker a chance to become aware of how they feel about an important aspect of their life. So this exercise is not a role play: it is for real.

As you work through this book and do the exercises, you may find yourselves getting lax about listening. Every now and then you could use this formal listening practice for your ordinary sharing.

Some further suggestions
Though it is best, if you are going to use the book in a group, to use it in the way I have outlined above (i.e. doing the exercises at home and using the group for sharing), I am occasionally asked about the possibility of a group of people meeting and doing the exercises at their meeting, and how much time each exercise needs. It is quite a difficult question to answer, because people differ quite a lot. Some need to spend much longer than others, and some are capable of reflecting more deeply than others. And in any case this book was originally written for people who were not able to get to group meetings, so its format does not always easily lend itself to being used in this way. However, here are some rough and ready suggestions: I hope they may be some help to you in designing your own course. They are only suggestions. And of course some exercises cannot by their nature be done at the meeting. I have taken that into account in what follows. I am assuming that it is for use by a group or groups of four people.

N.B. The exercises themselves need to be done in silence. Talking at this stage is liable to pull you away from *your* awareness, *your* perception, *your* experience.

Chapter 1 Hats exercise	• 10 mins. for making the list • 30 mins. for drawing and for naming the feelings that go with each 'hat'. Up to here it needs to be done in silence. • 7 mins. each for sharing.
Chapter 2 Expectations	• 40 mins. for the exercise (in silence). • 10 mins. each for sharing.
Chapter 3 Clock exercise	• Allow members an opportunity for a time to suggest itself, and for them to draw the hands in. • Then 15 mins. to write in their journal

about 'What time is it in my life?'
- 10 mins. for the sentence completions; complete each one at least three times. If anyone finishes early, they could expand on what they have written.
- 10+ mins. each for sharing (by reading out as much of what they have written as they wish, and then saying how they feel about what they've read out).

Chapter 4
Being present

- These exercises are best done at home in members' own time.
- If you use them in your meeting you will need to sample *each* of the ways of being present, because some people will find one way easier than another. Each person needs to be encouraged to use the one they find easiest. In your meeting you will need to:
- ensure everyone understands what the methods are by trying the 'static' ones for 5 or 10 mins. each. There is a tape 'Being Present' to help you with some of this. (All the tapes mentioned in these pages are obtainable from the address to be found on p. 207)
- then have 30 mins. in silence while you practise them. During this time people could choose whether to do so sitting still, or walking slowly outside. (The latter is easier if the district is quiet, but anywhere will do. This is after all simply an exercise in using sensory awareness to maintain your attention in the present.)
- Then 10 mins., still in silence, while people jot down what they were aware of through their senses, and what they noticed about their attention (when it wandered, in what way, what caused it to wander, what helped them to bring it back, etc.).
- 5 mins. each to share. *At all costs avoid theorising!* This was an exercise in *noticing* what happened, not discussing what ought to have happened.

This session may be the moment to suggest the idea of accountability, which is outlined in Chapter 16, p. 182.

Chapter 5
Notions of God

- Perhaps only 2 mins. for the drawing (it can help to do it quickly without 'thinking it out'; just start doodling about it straightaway without censoring it and see what happens. Be sure to include yourself also in your drawing).
- 5 mins. for sharing your feelings and memories aroused by your drawing.
- Then you could do the exercise with clay. *Note that this is not about making something*, but allowing the clay to bring something about how you are with God into your clearer awareness. In other words, in the sharing, focus on your awareness of the *process* as you played with the clay, not just how it ended up. Take 15 mins. for this.
- 5+ mins. for sharing what this brought to mind for you. Don't throw away your piece of clay until after you have shared your feelings. It may be that you want to keep it by you for a few days to absorb what it has raised for you.
- You could use the tape 'Open to the love of God' to end with.

This session could be the point at which you do the listening exercise on p. 175, to help to tighten up the discipline of listening in your group.

Chapter 6
Gospel event

- This is best done in your own time at home, since each person will be using a different event.
- If no-one in your group has experience of this kind of meditation you could use the tape 'Live a Gospel event' (note: those who are familiar with this method may find it cramps their style).
- If you just have a time of silence for each person to do their own meditation, allow

at least 30 mins. for that, plus
- 15 mins. for each person to write about what happened in their meditation in their journal.
- 5+ mins. each for sharing.

Chapter 7
Your story & psalm
- This is best done at home. It needs more time than could be available at your meeting.
- Allow *plenty* of time for each person to share their story and their psalm.

Chapter 8
Flaws & disabilities
- 15 mins. reflection
- 5+ mins. each for sharing (this could be longer depending on how free to speak people are feeling at this point in your group life).

Chapters 8 & 9 could be fitted into the same evening, if you wish.

Chapter 9
Loved by God
- Probably best done at home.
- By now you should have some idea how long you will need for sharing this.
- Then you could use the tape 'Open to the love of God'.

Chapter 10
Gift-naming
- Suggested timings for this are on p. 101.

(You *could*, if you wish, use Chapter 17 and its exercise here, before going on to Chapter 11.)

Chapter 11
Contemplative
visits
- Need to be done in your own time between group meetings.
- Probably 15 or 20 mins. for sharing.
- You could use the tape 'Open to the world's pain' which is a 20 min. meditation. Leave time for sharing the feelings of distress it may raise.

Chapter 12
Dreaming dreams
- Probably easier to do in your own time at home.
- But a member of your group *could* perhaps lead the first exercise on p. 124 at your meeting. If so, s/he needs to allow silence

for a few minutes wherever there is a row of dots in the text for people to jot their responses and feelings in their journals. This part of the session will probably take about 40 mins.

- Whether you do this exercise at home or in your group, when you come to the sharing it can be a good idea to change the 'atmosphere' a little as a reminder that sharing dreams has a different feel about it ('I have spread my dreams under your feet;' wrote W. B. Yeats, 'Tread softly because you tread on my dreams'.) If you have enough space, a group of 4 or 6 could lie face upwards on the floor with heads almost touching in the centre and your bodies like the spokes of a wheel. If space is limited, you could sit in a close circle round a candle in a darkened room. Be quiet in the presence of God for a minute or two. When someone is ready to share, the others listen, and perhaps respond as though the dream were already a reality. For example, if I were to share the dream I outlined on p. 7, the others might say how it would be for them or for someone they know if this were a reality at their church. The aim is to encourage the dreamer to articulate their dream and feel its power. If a dream has not yet come clear for you, just share what glimmerings or longings you have. Be flexible about the time each person needs.
- If you use one of the other two exercises in your group, allow at least 15 mins. reflection time – longer, if possible.

Chapter 13
Hear a call

- The first exercise needs to be done at home.
- At the beginning of your meeting, let there be an opportunity – for those who are ready to – to share their reflections from during the week. Take as much time as is required for this.
- Then you could use the Moses questions in

your group. The reader would need to pause for three or four minutes where the rows of dots are, for people to jot down their feelings and reactions (some gaps need to be longer than others – use your common sense). This will take at least 30 mins.

- Then you could have a time of silence while people look through their jottings and write down what strikes them about what they have written.
- For sharing, each person will need at least 10 mins.

Chapter 14
Face your fears

- The meditation will need 30 mins. (this could be best done at home).
- Share briefly, say 5 mins. each.
- Take a break and a breather.
- Then 20–30 mins. to write your deathbed letter to yourself.
- In the sharing each one could read out their letter, and then say how they felt as they read it: what does s/he notice about the experience of reading it aloud to the others? Do not rush this.

Chapter 15
Taking a step

- This exercise obviously has to be done in your own time, and may not fit in neatly with the dates of your group meetings. But there will almost certainly be something around this issue for you to share. The notes about accountability on pp. 182–3 may be helpful to you again at this point.

Chapter 16
The Church?

- One or two of you will already have taken the first step suggested in this exercise by starting your current group. How have you found it? Are there things about your experience of doing this that you could share with the others? (Be brave!)
- What about the second part of the exercise, asking your local church to 'commission' you for what you realise is your God-given

task just now? Is there a member of your group who is at this point? What could the rest of you do to encourage and support them? What sort of support would *they* like?

Chapter 17
The cost
(N.B. This chapter
could be used after
Chapter 10)

- 10–15 mins. for reflecting in your journal about the question.
- Say 5+ mins. each to share.
- This will be your last session. Take 10 mins. or so reflecting and jotting about what your personal next step needs to be: look again at the diagram on p. 6. Which thread(s) do you particularly need to focus on? Do you want to ask someone to hold you accountable for doing that?
- Each have a turn to share.
- To end, each person might be asked to look for and bring some object which s/he feels in some way is a symbol of herself or himself at the end of this course. Each one could have a turn to show the others the object and say in what way s/he feels it symbolises what has happened for her or him during the course. If you like, this could be part of a short act of worship in which each object is offered.
- Or, you could share informally on the following:

(From *Doorways to Christian Growth* by J. McMakin)

　　* I'm grateful for . . .
　　* I wish that . . .
　　* I'm disappointed about . . .
　　* I've learned . . .
　　* What I want to do now is . . .

Other Books by Francis Dewar

Called or Collared? An Alternative Approach to Vocation (London, SPCK 1991)

Give Yourself a Break (UK, Hunt & Thorpe 1992)

Invitations: God's Calling for Everyone (London, SPCK 1996)
This was originally conceived as a companion to *Live for a Change*; its subtitle is 'Stories and quotations to illuminate a journey'.

For further information about the tapes referred to in the text please write (enclosing an SAE) to:

JIJO Tapes
c/o The Warden
Education Resources Centre
The Old Deanery
Wells
BA5 2UG